Spiritual Alpha Female

Unleashing 9 Leadership Principles
from Proverbs 31

Rev. Dr. A'Shellarien Lang

Spiritual Alpha Female: Unleashing 9 Leadership Principles from Proverbs 31 Copyright © 2019 by Desakajo Publishing

4

Dedication

This book is dedicated to every woman who knows she is called to greater in her life and has decided that.... It's TIME.

Table of Contents

Foreword ....……...... 9

Introduction 11

Chapter 1: Spiritual Alpha Female in Proverbs 31 ..…..... 47

Spiritual Position of Attention: SPA.............................. 103

Chapter 2: **Principle # 1   U**pright Character

Queen Sheba/Authentic Leadership……...................... 105

SPA: Enlightenment of a Leader 119

Chapter 3: **Principle #2   N**ame Your Truth

Queen Michal/Emotional Intelligent Leadership 121

SPA: Endurance of a Leader... 135

Chapter 4: **Principle #3   L**ady on Your Own Terms

Queen Vashti/Transformational Leadership................... 137

SPA: Execution of a Leader.. 149

Chapter 5: **Principle #4   E**vident Integrity

Queen Bathsheba/Primal Leadership 151

SPA: Enrichment of a Leader 167

Chapter 6: **Principle #5   A**ccentuate Kindness

Queen Abigail/Path-Goal Leadership............................ 169

SPA: Elements of a Leader... 183

Chapter 7: **Principle #6   S**ervant Leader Heart

Queen Esther/Servant Leadership 185

SPA: Expansion of a Leader 197

Chapter 8 **Principle #7**   **H**umble Submission

Prophet Miriam/Situational Leadership 199

SPA: Examination of a Leader 211

Chapter 9 **Principle #8**   **E**ternal Gratefulness

Prophet Deborah/Steward Leadership 213

SPA: Expectation of a Leader 227

Chapter 10 **Principle #9**   **D**aughter of the Queen

Me/Spiritual Alpha Leadership 229

SPA: Enjoyment of a Leader 265

Afterword 267

References 279

Foreword

In a world where personal depreciation for public celebration is at an all-time high, it's often hard to find the courage to willfully display self-love. Demonstrations of self-love are interpreted as being vein, haughty or just down right EXTRA! In the words of Deborah Cox, "How did we get here?" Self-love is a mandatory staple in building self-esteem which is confidence in one's own worth or abilities. We all have been equipped with some ability granted to us through our heavenly Father. Some have the ability to sing, some can preach a roof of a church, and some people have the ability to mobilize communities into becoming great. Whatever the ability is, it should be celebrated. Some say there is a fine line between the celebration of one's self and bragging. I feel that we have lost sight of what it truly means to be celebrated.

During a workshop I conducted, as an icebreaker I asked the participants to say three amazing things about themselves. The room grew tense as each participant struggled through this exercise. One participant went on to say that she couldn't even think of anything good about herself and maybe if she were younger she could answer...WOW! Finally we got to a participant with a shred of self-love and she confidently gave her three answers. The room grew cold and you could see displeasure on others faces as she "glorified herself." This was a perfect example of how we so easily can find words that inflict self-hate but frown upon those who have chosen to muster up the strength to see the light inside of themselves even while fighting to peek through the dark clouds of depression, fear, anxiety, racism, sexism, classism and the list goes on and on.

Delve into these pages and explore the highs and lows of the "Spiritual Alpha Female." The woman that has endured the weight of societal inconsistencies yet continues to thrive. The woman who chooses to see the light within. The woman who chooses to live, when deep within her she fights whispers that encourage her to die. I know this woman all too well which is why I encourage you to read this book. Take the time to rediscover the beauty inside of you. Stand tall "Spiritual Alpha Female", I stand with you!

Desiree "Dezzie" Neal
Radio Personality & Media Correspondent

Introduction

Have you ever found yourself wondering why you shrink back into the fakeness of who you are instead of standing in the fullness of who you are? The fakeness of who you are is the diminished version of you that you willingly present as the true version of you. The fake you conforms to whatever the context calls for, complies with the current reality, and compromises true character. The fullness of who you are confirms your identity, challenges the status quo, and compels internal truth regardless of external influences. I often wonder why I do it myself. In the split second that it takes to decide to shrink into fakeness or to stand in fullness I find myself grieving the loss of who I know God called me to be whenever I choose to shrink. I remember being young knowing with blessed assurance that God called me to be a powerful girl in my own right. I had no way of articulating this sense of assurance that my "girlness" was divinely appointed to change the world. I had no way of knowing that my gender would become problematic on so many levels. I remember being 7 and someone gave me a Jehovah's Witness Bible and it was my favorite book. My favorite story came from 1 Kings 3:16-28 (NLT):

Sometime later two prostitutes came to the king to have an argument settled. [17] "Please, my lord," one of them began, "this woman and I live in the same house. I gave birth to a baby while she was with me in the house. [18] Three days later this woman also had a baby. We were alone; there were only two of us in the house. "But her baby died during the night when she rolled over on it. [20] Then she got up in the night and took my son from beside me while I was asleep. She laid her dead child in my arms and took mine to sleep beside her. [21] And in the morning when I tried to nurse my son, he was dead! But when I looked more closely in the morning light, I saw that it wasn't my son at all."[22] Then the other woman interrupted, "It certainly was your son, and the living child is mine." "No," the first woman said, "the living child is mine, and the dead one is yours." And so they argued back and forth before the king. [23] Then the king said, "Let's get the facts straight. Both of you claim the living child is yours, and each says that the dead one belongs to the other. [24] All right, bring me a sword." So a sword was brought to the king. [25] Then he said, "Cut the living child in two, and give half to one woman and half to the other!" [26] Then the woman who was the real mother of the living child, and who loved him very much, cried out, "Oh no, my lord! Give her the child— please do not kill him!" But the other woman said, "All right, he will be neither yours nor mine; divide him between us!" [27] Then the king said, "Do not kill the child, but give him to the woman who wants him to live, for she is his mother!"[28] When all Israel heard the king's decision, the people were in awe of the king, for they saw the wisdom God had given him for rendering justice.

This story resonated with me at a young age for the mere fact that God gave such wisdom to King Solomon. I remember understanding the love that the real mother had for her baby and being fascinated that God was so intricately involved in the lives of those that God loved. This story of these two women changed my life because I was drawn to the wisdom and the love. I made up my mind that I would ask God for wisdom like Solomon and love like that mother. The combination of wisdom and love makes a great leader. Proverbs 31 talks about a woman who used wisdom and love in her leadership. She is a wonderful example of what it means to stand in the fullness of femaleness with no consideration for shrinking back in life or in leadership.

When I reflect back on my understanding at 7, I am in awe of how I felt God present in my life at such a young age. I am clear that God has been with me from birth, however my consciousness about God's presence was very evident to me at 7. Here I am almost 7 times that age and still very conscious that God has divinely appointed my "girlness" to change the world. I can say with assurance that I never even considered shrinking back into the fakeness of who I was at 7. I consistently stood in the fullness of my blessed assurance that God infused power in my "girlness." There was never a split-second thought about having a choice. Here I stand in all of the fullness of my "womanness" with infused power by the Holy Spirit with the understanding that there are split seconds where I consciously shrink back in an attempt to protect myself or the man in my life whether that be my husband, my son, my brother, or my father. This begs the question, "why?" Why would women who have the blessed assurance that God dwells on the inside of them have split seconds when they make conscious choices to shrink back? Who has taught us to negate who we are in an effort to affirm who he is? Collette Dowling (1981) explains it this way:

The psychological need to avoid independence-the "wish to be saved" is quite probably the most important issue facing women today. We were brought up to depend on a man and to feel naked and frightened without one. We were taught to believe that as women we cannot stand alone, that we are too fragile, too delicate, needful of protection. So that now, in these enlightened days, when our intellects tell us to stand on our own two feet, unresolved emotional issues drag us down. At the same time that we yearn to be fetterless and free, we also yearn to be taken care of. We have only one real shot at liberation and that is to emancipate ourselves from within. Personal, psychological dependency-the deep wish to be taken care of by others-is the chief force holding women down today. When we grow up and stop hiding behind the patronage of someone we choose to think of as "stronger"; we begin making decisions based on our own values-not our husbands or parents. Freedom demands that we become authentic, true to ourselves. When we begin the process of separating from our authority figures to stand on our own two feet, we discover that the values we thought were our own are not. This dizzying loss of old and outmoded support structures-beliefs we don't believe anymore-can mark the beginning of true freedom. But the fact that it's frightening can send us scurrying into retreat-back to where it's safe, familiar, known.

Being a woman who rests in the fullness of who you truly are can be scary. Women are taught to be dependent yet independent at the same time. You have the spectrum of beliefs around a woman's place, a woman's voice, and a woman's self-directed life. Dowling (1981) introduced in the 80's what she calls the Cinderella Complex-a network of largely repressed attitudes and fears that keep women in a kind of half-light, retreating from the full use of their minds and creativity. Here we are over 30 years later and like Cinderella, women today are still waiting for something external to transform their lives. Dowling raised a viable point about the internal struggle with independence and dependence. Independence, dependence, or a combination of both is a choice that every woman must come to terms with. None of the choices are bad, what is bad is choosing one and trying to live the other. If you choose to be dependent on a man and allow him to make all of your decisions for you that is your choice to make. If you choose to never depend on a man that is your choice as well. If by chance you choose to live somewhere in the middle that choice is also yours to make. If you want to be independent yet you choose a man that requires complete dependence, you exemplify what Dowling is talking about. Your internal struggle with dependence or independence is manifested by your words saying independence while your choice of companion says dependence. The struggle is real for many women especially those who are attempting to ingest a biblical model that is marginalizing on some levels.

God gives us freewill however the male directed narrative that many women have been acculturated and indoctrinated with says the contrary. Also know that the "I don't need a man" narrative from women is just as dangerous as the male directed narrative. I have encountered many women who have worked tirelessly on being internally dependent on God yet externally dependent on themselves. They are very sure that they are powerful, intelligent, beautiful women yet they wrestle with the societal construct of female dependency on a man. Dowling is correct in that women struggle with listening to their head that tells them to stand strong and speak their truth or yielding to their unresolved broken heart that tells them to sit and be quiet. It is a hard place to be and a sad space to live, move and have your being. Generation after generation of women have wrestled with this place and space. It reminds me of a story that I created called Raise Your Branches:

There was a mother tree who was talking to her daughter tree. She said sweetheart you have been wondrously created by Creator God, you are beautiful, strong, and powerful. You have great purpose here on the earth don't let anyone tell you otherwise. As they were having that conversation a male tree began to tell the mother tree that she was subject to the male trees and could do nothing without their permission. The male tree told her that the Creator made the male trees to be in charge and they have decided that female trees are not a good reflection of the Creator's goodness and from now on they need to monitor how high their branches spread because they cannot be higher or better than the male trees. The mother tree told the male tree, that what he was saying was not true we are just as important to the Creator as the male trees. You cannot limit our greatness like that. The Creator put us here for a reason and we are proud of that. The male tree got together with some other male trees and openly and intentionally began to hinder the water supply of the mother tree and she eventually died. The daughter tree believed her mother tree and watched what happened to her as she stood up for herself. The daughter tree went on to have a daughter tree and told her the same thing her mother tree told her but added you must always remember how special you are even though you have to limit how high you spread your branches because the male trees will hurt you if you don't. The granddaughter tree was confused and wondered why. Her mother tree told her the story of the fate of her grandmother tree and so she understood and complied. This granddaughter tree watched how the other female trees complied as well. She went on to have a daughter tree and told her everything that her mother tree told her. That great granddaughter tree said wait why are we letting the male trees tell us what to do if the Creator never said that? The granddaughter tree told her what happened to her great grandmother tree and still she said why are we letting them have the power to tell us who we are? We can come together and take our power back and spread our branches as high and as beautifully as we were originally created to do. All female trees will know and declare that they are equally loved and valued by the Creator. There were other female trees some young like her, some older like her mother tree, and some even older like her great grandmother tree that agreed with her and began to say so. The other female trees shared that they always believed that they were loved and valued by the Creator just like the male trees but were told by their mother trees to stay in their place. They talked about how they told themselves to hold on to the truth even though they were forced to live a lie. The granddaughter tree listened to the great granddaughter tree and all of the other female trees shared their stories and said today we take our power back. Today we no longer tell our daughter trees to accept and internalize the lie that they were not created with the same love and value as male trees. From that day on the conversation between mother tree and daughter tree and the conversation that the female trees had with themselves was forever changed.

The tree analogy is a snippet into the lives of women throughout the ages. These women have held on to the belief that they were created in the image and likeness of God. Even with that knowledge they have allowed the men in their lives to dictate who they are, how they think, and what their potential is for greatness. When they yielded to the notion that men are right, like other women trees, they made the split-second decision to shrink back into fakeness instead of standing in fullness.

Beloved, I am convinced that the first woman's experience with being loved and then being blamed for the fall of humankind made a place for the split second decision to shrink back in fakeness instead of standing in the fullness of who she was. The *Us* in "Let Us make humankind in our image and in our likeness" (Genesis 1:26 NIV) is the fullness of femaleness in perfect combination with the fullness of maleness. I am a firm believer that the *Us* in the creation story is the real story. The first human in Genesis appears to have been the partialness of maleness with the partialness of femaleness on the inside of him. When *They* saw that it was not good for the partialness of maleness and the partialness of femaleness to dwell in one body, *They* put the male to sleep and took the female out of him so that he could experience the external manifestation of the fullness of who he already had on the inside of him. Genesis 2:23 shares the man's response to God at his first encounter with the woman: "This is now bone of my bones and flesh of my flesh; she shall be called woman for she was taken out of man". Genesis 3:12 shares the man's response to God after they ate the fruit: "The woman whom you gave to be with me". The man welcomed the woman at their first encounter and declared that she was a part of him. The Bible does not say how long it was between their first physical encounter and their disobedience experience in the Garden. What we do know is that the woman was blamed for what they did and was dismissed and demonized. The "bone of his bone and flesh of his flesh" had become the "thorn in his flesh". The cycle of abuse for the demonization of women began in the garden. The Bible shares many stories of violence against and hatred of women. The hatred of women frames the Bible in the Genesis 3 story where she is blamed for the fall of humankind and the Revelation 12 story where she is pursued by the Great Dragon. Our encounter with the Bible is similar to that of Adam, what began as bone of our bone experience soon become a thorn in our flesh experience. The question for many women is how do I embrace a narrative that dismisses and demonizes me based solely on a male interpretation of what happened in the beginning of creation? What happened to the redeeming blood of Christ that was supposed to restore humankind back to right standing? The original relationship between the woman and the man was a partnership. The hierarchical misrepresentation of "how God intended" for the female and male relationship was superimposed into the text.

The Bible shares the man's first encounter with the woman. It gives his response and not hers. I often wonder what she said when she saw him for the first time. I wonder what *They* said to her before she was presented to him. It is possible that *They*, the fullness of femaleness and the fullness of maleness, gave her wisdom and love to live, move, and have her being as a human female version of *Them*. It is possible that the fullness of femaleness gave Divine guidance to her as she wrestled with her creation, her purpose, and her future. Unfortunately, we will never know what *They* said to her. What we do know is that the male narrative erased the fullness of femaleness from the Divine picture. Raver (1998) said we must always remember that *Elohim* is Goddess and God together, the feminine and masculine joining to form the Infinite One. The Bible began with a powerful acknowledgement of the dual nature of the Source of Being, but by chapter two of Genesis, *Elohim* was thought of as singular and male. "He" was called "God," and when Eve did not obey "Him," she was cursed with male domination and the Divine Feminine shared Eve's fate. Raver helps us to see that the Feminine Divine was present at the beginning of the sixth day and dismissed by the end of the sixth day. Tragically, the *Us* was turned into a *He* and glorified while *She* was dismissed and demonized even though the Bible gives male and female images of God. According to Meyers (2000):

> The direct or indirect gynomorphic images for God do not, of course, necessarily indicate a belief in a female deity any more than the andromorphic images constitute evidence that the Israelites believed that YHWH was literally male. To be sure, post-biblical theological tradition, heavily influenced by the prominent "God the father" language of early Judaism and Christianity, has certainly asserted conviction that the deity is male. Yet the presence of both female and male images of God in the Hebrew Bible should open the question not so much of whether God is female and/or male, but rather about the nature of metaphoric language for God. Because God is so utterly Other, God's nature transcends the ability of humans to express it. The biblical writers used the language of human behavior, female or male as appropriate, to convey their ideas about YHWH. More often than not, such metaphoric language appears in biblical poetry, where

it is meant to cause an emotional impact rather than depict a concrete reality.

Contrary to what we have been taught, the fullness of femaleness compliments the fullness of maleness. Neither female nor male function to their potential while they operate in their partiality. The partial you is the fake you. The truth is that the woman was created in response to the "not good" that *They* declared as they observed the man being alone. She was created to make the "not good, good." My sister, you were created to make the not good, good. Imagine how different your life would be right now if you were told that when you were a little girl. Imagine how different our daughters, granddaughters, and great granddaughters lives will be when we tell them they were created to make the not good, good.

I often wonder if women understand that when they shrink back they are attempting to fully function in their partiality. It is not unlike the difference in functioning as a girlfriend or a wife. A girlfriend has partial access to a full relationship with a man while a wife has full access to a full relationship with a man. I hear you saying, "What is the difference?" Well, Beloved, the difference is covenant. While some may say that commitment is commitment whether girlfriend or wife, the truth is covenant, the internally driven desire to honor your words with actions that match, makes all the difference. Covenant is the game changer in your relationships with men as well as your relationship with yourself. Have you ever considered whether or not you have a covenant with yourself? Today, I challenge you to ask yourself am I internally driven to honor myself through my words with actions to match them? What does it look like to dishonor yourself? Do you live an unfulfilled life because you believe you must live up to what people say? Do you silence yourself in an effort to go along to get along? Is it that you never pursue your dreams of leadership because your man would be left behind? Is it that you create goals around a man who has yet to find out who you really are? Do you limit yourself and your leadership abilities because you are afraid that reaching your destiny means leaving him behind? It is sad to think that our creation was for naught because we choose to live below who God called us to be in pursuit of men who have yet to discover who they are let alone honor who we are.

Beloved, womanhood is an honor. The mere fact that *They* fashioned us after coming to the realization that it was not good for "man" to be alone, speaks to the attention to detail that *They* put into us. While I believe the first human being was male and female like *Them*, it is evident that there needed to be a separate human form for them to function to their greatest potential based on the limitations of being human instead of Divine. Unfortunately, we will never know what *They* truly had in store for the human female version of *Them*. What we do know is that she was sacrificed like a lamb before the slaughterer to take the fall of humankind. The enmity that Genesis 3:15 speaks about has fueled the fire of sexism in the church and in society. While the text is specifically talking to the serpent when it says, "And I will put enmity between you and the woman, and between your seed and her seed; He shall bruise your head, And you shall bruise His heel" that enmity intended to between the woman and the serpent has been transposed to being enmity between the female and the male. אֵיבָה *ebah* enmity is defined as hostility/hatred. I am convinced that the same serpent that hates women in Genesis 3 is the same serpent in Revelations 12:17 (KJV),

"And the dragon was enraged with the woman, and he went to make war with the rest of her offspring, who keep the commandments of God and have the testimony of Jesus Christ." I am convinced that you must know the end of the story to understand the beginning. The serpent in Revelation 12 was angry with her and understood that she was being protected. What better way to get back at her than by causing him to dishonor her. After they both ate, God questioned him about his actions and his response was, "The woman you gave to be with me, she gave me of the tree, and I ate." (Genesis 3:12 KJV) Her response to God's question was to blame the serpent. The serpent's punishment was hatred from her and her seed and towards her and her seed. God's punishment to her was that she would desire the man and he would rule over her. God's punishment to the man was that the ground would be cursed and he would have to work hard to yield from it. I hear you saying what does any of that have to do with leadership? Well Beloved, leadership is about relationship. There is no leadership without followship. The barriers that exists in relationship building for women stem from the first relationship that Genesis presents.

Northhouse (2013) defines leadership as a process that is not a trait or characteristic that resides in the leader, but rather a transactional event that occurs between the leader and the followers. Process implies that a leader affects and is affected by followers. It emphasizes that leadership is not a linear, one-way event, but rather an interactive event. Northhouse gives a wonderful definition of the dynamics of leadership. The emphasis is on influence. Women in leadership have been influenced by what they have been told about being a woman in a man's world. They either embrace it or reject it and find themselves either elevated for compliance or demoted for non-compliance. Men have many models of leadership in the Bible to pattern their lives after. There are a plethora of snippets of dialogue that demonstrate leadership from a male perspective. Unfortunately, women are very limited in their snippets of leadership from a woman's perspective. How we see things is limited to our frame of reference. What we see and what we do not see is dependent upon how we are conditioned to see whether that be what lies right in the open, what lies on the sidelines, and/or what is not even there. Gebara (1974) says:

Human wisdom enters into a power struggle between the sexes. An analysis of gender reveals that control over knowledge and the accepted wisdom is truly men's power and privilege. Women are intruders, usurpers of something not belonging to them, and they do wrong when they desire to know, and as an answer to that wrong society must restore harmony by chastisement, silence, torture, or death. In this way the hierarchy of the world and humanity is maintained.

Gebrara lifts a valuable point in that human wisdom is a power struggle. It is up to us to take the power back by reading and reinterpreting the Bible to correct what has been distorted. There are many women in leadership in the Bible and when we take the time to lift them from the pages we can learn a lot. Keen (1991) says since the beginning of "his-story" there has been a largely untold "her-story" of exceptional women who transcend the deadening status quo and came alive to the special pain and indignities that accompany the womanly condition. Keen is right in that the "her-story" needs to be lifted and heard. This book is designed to do just that. The impulse for some women is to get their power back through learning the truth and then living their lives. My impulse is to gain my power back and then share that power with other women who will then share it with those that they lead. Leadership is nothing without followship.

When it comes to impulse control it is paramount for leaders to understand that their discipline or lack thereof has a direct impact on how their followers behave. Impulse control has a lot to do with how we handle our difficult thoughts and emotions. I have a lot of emotion around the silence of women in leadership in the Bible. God has called me to a place of influence and I must take responsibility for the way that others are affected by my emotional response. David and Congleton (2015) shared that it is impossible to block out difficult thoughts and emotions; Effective leaders are mindful of their inner experiences but not caught in them. They know how to free up their internal resources and commit to actions that align with their values. Influence can be good as well as bad. It is my desire to take my passion around lifting "her-story" to influence women in leadership in a positive way. We are in the pages, our voices are present, and as we glean from the women who have been pushed to the periphery of the leadership dialogue we will be forever changed.

Woman will be empowered and infused with knowledge to lead other women out of silence into a place where they too will speak their truth. Northouse (2013) said:

> Leadership involves influence. It is concerned with how the leader affects followers. Influence is the sine qua non of leadership. Without influence, leadership does not exist. Leadership occurs in groups. Groups are the context in which leadership takes place. Leadership involves influencing a group of individuals who have a common purpose. Leaders direct their energies toward individuals who are trying to achieve something together.

Northouse is focused on both the leader and the follower. A perfect example of that is Deborah in the Bible, she could only lead if people were following. Deborah called for Barak to lead and he would not go without her. Her influence was in full operation and it ushered in a wave of loyalty that exemplifies true leadership. The interesting thing about influence is that there are times when the influence is forced upon people and other times when the influence is embraced by the people. Some people have no choice to follow while others choose to follow. The leader holds as much power as the followers give them. Effective leaders lead people who choose to follow. In Deborah's case the people chose to follow her. She exemplified the transactional event that happens between leaders and followers.

There is an unnamed woman in leadership who speaks words of wisdom and love to her son in Proverbs 31. The only thing we know about her is that she is King Lemuel's mother. For the purposes of this book we will call her Queen Mother. Queen Mother in Proverbs 31 was a woman of great wisdom and had great influence in the life of her son. There is a story in the Bible that talks about a King who loved, honored, and respected his Queen Mother and sat her in the place of honor. 1 Kings 2:19 (NRSV) shares the story of Solomon honoring his mother; "So Bathsheba went to King Solomon to speak to him on behalf of Adonijah. The king rose to meet her and bowed down to her then sat on his throne and had a throne brought for the king's mother and she sat on his right." What does it mean that Solomon whom the Bible calls the wisest King, made a place for his mother on his right side? The right is a reference to both proximity to God and the position of power and influence.

The Bible makes many references to the right hand of God and Jesus sitting at the right hand of God. Psalm 118:15-16 (NRSV) says, "There are glad songs of victory in the tents of the righteous: The right hand of the Lord does valiantly; the right hand of the Lord is exalted; the right hand of the Lord does valiantly." Romans 8:33-35 (NRSV) says, "Who will bring any charge against God's elect? It is God who justifies. Who is to condemn? It is Christ Jesus who died, yes, who was raised, who is at the right hand of God, who indeed intercedes for us. Who will separate us from the love of Christ? The right hand of God is powerful and has great influence and Jesus sitting at the right hand of God comes with power and influence." When we mess up Jesus uses the power and influence that was given to Him to intercede on our behalf. There is a reason that King Solomon made the choice to rise to greet his mother (love), bow to her (honor), and place a throne to the right of his (respect). He was the King, yet he yielded to the power and influence of his mother. The book of Proverbs is attributed to King Solomon and shares his words of wisdom. Proverbs 1:1-9 (NKJV) says:

The proverbs of Solomon the son of David, King of Israel: To know wisdom and instruction, to perceive the words of understanding, to receive the instruction of wisdom, justice, judgement, and equity; To give prudence to the simple, to the young man knowledge and discretion- A wise man will hear and increase learning and a man of understanding will attain wise counsel to understand a proverb and an enigma, the words of the wise and their riddles. The fear of the Lord is the beginning of knowledge, but fools despise wisdom and instruction. My son, hear the instruction of your father, and do not forsake the law of your mother; For they will be a graceful ornament on your head, and chains about your neck.

Solomon emphasized the value in embracing wisdom in the first seven verses of his book. What stood out the most to me was what he said about mothers in verse 8, my son, hear the instruction of your father and do not forsake the law תּוֹרָה (Torah) of your mother. Proverbs 6:20 echoes the very same thing when it comes to the mother. The first five books of the Bible are called the Torah. The

Torah sets the tone for how those who honor the Bible live, move, and have their being. Solomon said hear your father and do not forsake the Torah that your mother teaches you. The mother played a major role in imparting God's wisdom to the children and King Solomon reinforced that.

Like King Solomon, King Lemuel yielded to the power and influence of his mother's teaching. Proverbs 31 is where we find the Queen Mother sharing a phenomenal woman that she recommends for her son, yet she has been minimized to a housewife and mother. While there is nothing wrong with being a housewife and a mother, there is something wrong with not acknowledging the fullness of who she is as a woman, as a leader. The Queen Mother's description of this woman who exemplifies leadership at its best can be found in Proverbs 31:10-31(NKJV):

Who can find a virtuous wife? For her worth *is* far above rubies. The heart of her husband safely trusts her; so he will have no lack of gain. She does him good and not evil all the days of her life. She seeks wool and flax, and willingly works with her hands. She is like the merchant ships, she brings her food from afar. She also rises while it is yet night, and provides food for her household, and a portion for her maidservants. She considers a field and buys it; From her profits she plants a vineyard. She girds herself with strength and strengthens her arms. She perceives that her merchandise is good, and her lamp does not go out by night. She stretches out her hands to the distaff and her hand holds the spindle. She extends her hand to the poor, yes, she reaches out her hands to the needy. She is not afraid of snow for her household, for all her household is clothed with scarlet. She makes tapestry for herself; Her clothing is fine linen and purple. Her husband is known in the gates, when he sits among the elders of the land. She makes linen garments and sells them and supplies sashes for the merchants. Strength and honor are her clothing; She shall rejoice in time to come. She opens her mouth with wisdom, and on her tongue is the law of kindness. She watches over the ways of her household and does not eat the bread of idleness. Her children rise up and call her blessed; Her husband also and he praises her: Many daughters have done well, but you excel them all. Charm is deceitful and beauty is passing, But a woman who fears the LORD, she shall be praised. Give her of the fruit of her hands, and let her own works praise her in the gates.

The Queen Mother describes a woman I call a Spiritual Alpha Female. The Spiritual Alpha Female is not afraid to step into the fullness of who she is called by God to be. She is fully aware of the limitations placed on her access to lead by religious and societal constructs. She is well aware of the backlash that she will get from other women who sit uncomfortably in the quietness of their lives as they go along to get along in their minimized leadership role. She is very aware of the internal struggle with the voice that calls her to stand tall in the fullness of the leader she is born to be in the face of the voice that tells her to sit back and let him lead. She is fully present with herself knowing that God has given her the grace and the grit to live, move, and have her being in the fullness of her leadership. God is her foundation, faith is her framework, and leadership is her future.

The Alpha Female, on the other hand, has been sexualized and portrayed as one who is intimidating to men as well as women. She is seen in a negative light as one who is not afraid to speak her mind, put people in their place, and command the environment that she inhabits. While it is true that she is a powerhouse in her own right, it is also true that because she is a female she is demonized while men with the same qualities are celebrated. Unfortunately, the Proverbs 31 woman has been minimized to what she has to offer instead of being celebrated for all of who she is. The Spiritual Alpha Female has 9 specific characteristics that can be drawn from Queen Mother's description of the perfect woman. She is: A confident woman, a powerful woman, an innovative woman, a wise woman, a kind woman, a surrendered woman, a loving woman, a woman of great faith, and a woman who honors God with the fullness of who she is. I have taken these nine characteristics and pulled out 9 leadership principles: Upright Character, Name Your Truth, Lady on Your Own Terms, Evident Integrity, Accentuate Kindness, Servant Leader Heart, Humble Submission, Eternal Gratefulness, and Daughter of the Queen. The nine leadership principles combined with the nine characteristics lay the foundation for nine leadership styles: Authentic Leadership, Emotionally Intelligent Leadership, Transformational Leadership, Primal Leadership, Path-Goal Leadership, Servant Leadership, Situational Leadership, Steward Leadership, and Spiritual Alpha Leadership. The portrait of the Spiritual Alpha Female in Proverbs 31 is a collage of a great leader that every woman can glean from. According to Bishop Vashti M. McKenzie, the first woman Bishop in the history of the African Methodist Episcopal Church (2002):

As women, we are sometimes defined by one role: mother, daughter, teacher, executive, wife, sister, architect, or pharmacist, rather than as a collage of many women kneaded into one like yeast kneaded into fresh dough. We see ourselves as one image, one composition, one photograph, one kodak moment at a time. We present ourselves to the world as one woman at a time letting all the other women inside us starve for attention. These other women inside of us are hidden by the demands of work, standing in the constant shadow of our responsible selves, taking a backseat to the woman who must work to eat, give to live, pay bills, and hold up her end of the relationship.

Each woman within our personal collage is a chapter in the story of our lives, and each of these women contributes to the others. One woman doesn't threaten another, since each one is necessary to our story and one woman connects us the next woman. Each represents a significant stage, moment, or development in life, but we will not get the entire picture until we step back and view the collage as a whole. One piece of the collage does not tell the whole story.

The fullness of who we are is the collage that Bishop McKenzie is referring to. Being a woman is a phenomenal blessing that comes with many facets. The woman that Proverbs 31 talks about is a collage of the perfect woman, the perfect leader who stands in the fullness of who she is.

Now while our brothers wrestle with their own ability to stand in the fullness of who they are, this book is designed to help women in leadership not shrink back to their fake selves in an effort to accommodate the societal construct that has attempted to orchestrate their place. There is a place for women who no longer desire to conform to the construct that dictates where they can and should live, move, and have their being. There are women who have

42

an innate ability to lead, the ability to create, the ability to manage well, the ability to bring greatness forth, and the ability to do all that they are told a woman should not do by men as well as women. Women have struggled with their interpersonal relationships with other women, struggled with leading as a woman, struggled with relating to men on a personal and professional level, and struggled with holding on to themselves in all four areas. The struggles that women experience when it comes to leadership are real and relevant. I have come across many books about leadership and have found very few that are geared specifically to women from a non-biased, non-"stay in your place and lead", and you don't have to be like a man to be good leader perspective. It is my intention to empower women to stand in the fullness of who they are, trusting in the fullness of who God called them to be to lead with excellence using the principles that Proverbs 31 teaches.

This book that you hold in your hands will enable you to unleash your Spiritual Alpha Female as you unveil the true leadership in the Proverbs 31 woman. In this book I lift 9 Women who I consider Spiritual Alpha Females: Queen of Sheba, Queen Michal, Queen Vashti, Queen Bathsheba, Queen Abigail, Queen

43

Esther, Prophet Miriam, Prophet Deborah, and You. Each woman embodies the nine characteristics and masters one of the nine leadership principles and one of nine leadership styles. Whatever aspect of this Spiritual Alpha Female that pertains to you, honor her. Use this book to accentuate the leader in you that already exists. The leadership of the Proverbs 31 woman has been minimized and unfortunately many women in leadership have been minimized as well. This book is designed to maximize your leadership ability and potential through the life and lens of this phenomenal portrait of a woman. At the end of each chapter is the Call To Spiritual Position of Attention. In the military, service members come to the position of attention to show respect to the one speaking. For the Spiritual Alpha Female, we come to the spiritual position of attention to show respect to God as God speaks to us. It is coming to a spiritual internal space where we turn to God with our whole heart and really listen to what God wants to reveal to us. The Call to Spiritual Position of Attention at the close of each chapter lifts the leadership principle and leadership style that we can embody as a Spiritual Alpha Female. Use this book to develop the leader you desire to be. Use this book to empower yourself and other women in your life. Use it individually or in a group. No matter what you decide to use this book to do, let it change your life and leadership for the better.

Chapter One

Spiritual Alpha Female Proverbs 31 Woman

I am a woman who is fully present within myself with the understanding that God created me as a woman for a Divine reason. I am fully aware that my understanding of *They* (Let *Us* create humans in *Our* image, in *Our* likeness, male and female created *They* them) in the creation story helps to frame my life. I am created in the image and likeness of the Female Divine who serves as the female fullness of *They*. She is ever present in my life regardless of whether or not She is acknowledged, honored, or celebrated. I am a woman and the *Spirit* on the inside of me is female. I have spent my life trying to superimpose the patriarchal system of the exclusive maleness of God and it annihilates the glory in which I was created as a woman. Genesis shares the story of the creation of humankind. The beginning of the story is a male human being. *They* said that it was not good for this "male" to be alone. *They* decided to have a physical manifestation of female and male, both were created in the

47

image and likeness of *Them*. I believe that I am created in the image and likeness of the female fullness of God and the partial maleness of God. God exceeds our limited ability to comprehend. What we think we know is a snippet into the fullness of who God is. I dishonor the fullness of *They*, male and female, if I negate that my reflection as a woman is Divine. So much has happened between what we were taught about the beginning and today. I am convinced that who I am as a woman is wrapped up in who God created me to be. It is up to me to seek God beyond the people who are presenting God to me.

There is a biblical presentation that says who you are is wrapped up in the man that you are connected to. You are the daughter of, the wife of, the sister of, the mother of........ This association with men has infiltrated our sense of self. Our identity has been meshed with the men in our lives. Unfortunately, the Bible reinforces this notion that our identity is connected to a man. I am convinced that women have been indoctrinated with this idea that they are who they are based on the man that they are connected to. This indoctrination makes it difficult for women to step out of the shadow of the man and into the fullness of who she really is. Women from all walks of life have struggled with coming to terms with who they really are, what they really want, and how well they really lead. The mental, spiritual, and emotional health of women has been hindered for a long time. Jeremiah 8: 11, 21-22 (NASB) speaks to this very thing when it says:

> They heal the brokenness of the daughter of My people superficially, Saying, 'Peace, peace,' But there is no peace. For the brokenness of the daughter of my people I am broken; I mourn, dismay has taken hold of me. Is there no balm in Gilead? Is there no physician there? Why then has not the health of the daughter of my people been restored?

Jeremiah is addressing God's concern for the mental, spiritual, and emotional health of women. While there are women who are blessed to be in mentally, spiritually, and emotionally healthy spaces, there are far more who do not live, move, and have their being in a healthy space. The question becomes can you be truly healthy in one if you are not truly healthy in all? Where you find yourself is your truth. There is no universal truth for all women. There is a spiritual continuum of health that women may or may not have the strength to assess. There is a mental continuum of health that women may or may not be able to address. Finally, there is an emotional continuum of health that women may or may not be able to manage. I have found that the emotional development of women is something like this: Little girls are free to be themselves without inhibition; Elementary girls begin to explore changing who they are to accommodate boys; Teenage girls begin to experience the result of being themselves in relation to the boys they are interested in; Young adult women have learned from their teenage years that they need to minimize who they are to keep the peace with the young man of their choice; Adult women wrestle with their choice to minimize who they are and long for the freedom to be themselves; And older women regret their choice to minimize who they are and take steps to walk in the fullness of who they want to be. This emotional movement is not prescriptive in that every woman does not follow this pattern. There are some women who discover early that they have minimized who they are, there are some women who go through life and never become emotionally present enough to realize that they have minimized who they are, and there are some women who never minimize who they are for a man. No matter

50

where you find yourself, the Proverbs 31 woman may resonate with some aspect of who you are.

Proverbs 31 opens with Queen Mother telling her son not to entertain the wrong kind of woman and closes with giving guidance about pursuing the right kind of woman. We are challenged with the Proverbs 31 woman because she is not identified and she never speaks. She is a portrait of a woman who exemplifies the fullness of womanhood. She is fully present within herself and handles her life on her terms. She loves her husband and children well, buys, sells, cooks, delegates, sews, and mentors. She is a leader, a business woman, a seamstress, a craftswoman, and a coach. With all of that, she never speaks. We do not know her struggle, we do not know her pain, and we do not know the many challenges that she faces as she leads. So often we look at women around us and assume that they are strong and handle everything that life throws at them. Unlike the Proverb 31 woman, we have the ability to speak our truth. We have the ability to share our struggles with other women. This book is designed to draw you into the sisterhood so that you have a safe space to mentor and be mentored by women who have struggles as well. We are overcomers by the word of our testimony. My sister, you have overcome a life of preparation, position, and promise to get where you are and it is time to pull a sister up with you. Let us use the fullness of the Proverbs 31 woman to learn more about ourselves and each other.

This portrait of a woman in Proverbs 31 has been used to make women feel inferior, inadequate, and not good enough. It is almost impossible to live up to the lifestyle of this woman. Attempting to live up to this portrait of a woman would leave us exhausted, overworked, overextended, and not very good at self-care. I propose that we use the leadership principles in this portrait of a woman to become Spiritual Alpha Females. We can take the elements of the portrait that we want to internalize and glean from the rest. Proverbs 31 has been presented as sacredly prescriptive of the perfect woman and it may be a hard adjustment for some to see it as a portrait of a fictitious woman. Savina Teubal (1990) shares that sacred writings serve to indoctrinate people into a particular belief. So we must ask ourselves in whose interest would sanctioning the subordination of women and their enslavement be most advantageous? She goes on to say perhaps the most profound disservice perpetrated on humanity has been the disassociation of woman from her own female religious experience. Teubal speaks to the indoctrination of Proverbs 31 and it sheds light on the truth that women were not given opportunity to speak their own truth about Proverbs 31. The misappropriation of the value of Proverbs 31 has unfortunately caused a division among women who should be on the same side.

Spiritual Alpha Females are not in competition with each other. The spiritual overpowers the Alpha which allows the female to be elevated to the place of excellence that she was created to occupy. There is a dividing line that exists among various groups of women. Specifically in America, there is a distinct dividing line between African American women and European American women. My time in seminary gave me the grace and space to look at the intentional implementation of division among these two groups. While I am aware that women from non-European descent also have challenges with other groups of women, I believe that the overall tension that is felt in America stems from this particular strained relationship. Leadership becomes a major challenge as a whole as long as these two groups continue to dishonor each other. I would like to suggest that there has been psychological violence that has occurred within the lives of women who have struggled to find a better way. Jon Paul (2003) defines violence as not only acts of individual physical aggression, but also to social and linguistic systems of exclusion and collective coercion, degradation, or destruction of property, persons, and the environment. Psychological violence happens during the intellectually driven emotional process going on in women individually and collectively. I believe that women have internalized conditioning that repeats itself generation after generation that leads to a continuous psychological cycle of self-oppression and disconnection from other women. I believe that when women come together on one accord the result will be liberation one generation at a time until the distortion of gender and role is corrected. Unfortunately, the patriarchal system has synthesized value of the women's role and value of the women's personhood when role should not determine personhood. The patriarchal system portrays the portrait of a woman in Proverbs 31 as a "true" woman. The unfair portrayal sets women up to attempt to live up to an unattainable goal. The misinterpretation and the misuse of the Bible perpetuates the psychological violence that women experience.

African American women were fed an oppressive patriarchal story that dealt with sexism, classism, and racism that was imposed upon them by other women. European American women were fed an oppressive patriarchal story that dealt with sexism, classism, and the imposition of racism on to other women. Both groups had to find a safe space within a society that looked down on them because of their gender. These women were conditioned to perform in the role that was set for them and eventually internalized it so well that they looked down on any woman who wanted to be liberated from it. Here we are generations later and many women have no idea that the intentional division did not come from them, their mothers, their grandmothers, nor from the Creator, Sustainer, and Preserver of our lives.

European American women had to contend with the intentional annihilation of their personhood because of her gender through the use of the Malleus Maleficarum (Hammer of Witches). It was written in 1486 by Heinrich Kramer and Jacob Sprenger to instruct magistrates how to find, question, and prosecute witches. They were members of the Dominican Order and Inquisitors for the Catholic Church. This document was submitted to the University of

Cologne's Faculty of Theology in 1487. 14 editions were published in 1520 and 16 in 1669. The first English edition came in 1584. The main grip that it had on society and the detriment that it caused to women in particular is that it linked heresy to witchcraft during the Inquisition. The Inquisition was an ecclesiastical tribunal established by Pope Gregory IX in 1232. It was formed to suppress heresy and became notorious for the use of torture. In 1542 the papal Inquisition was re-established to combat Protestantism. Anytime anyone questioned the Catholic Church and its doctrine, they were considered heretics. Heretics were killed and people were terrified. At the height of the Malleus Maleficarum's popularity, it was surpassed in public notoriety only by the Bible. Estimates of the death toll during the Inquisition worldwide range from 600,000 to as high as 9,000,000 over a 250 year period. Nearly all of the accused were women. The influence was even felt in the New World with the Salem Witch Trials in Massachusetts. The document posited women as weak and susceptible to adhering to Satan's influence. The institution of the inquisitions was abolished in the early 19th century. The fundamental beliefs of the inquisitors survived as part of the Roman Curia. In 1908 the group was renamed the Supreme Sacred Congregation of the Holy Office. In 1965 it became the Congregation of the Doctrine of Faith. The embedded effects of that imposed belief can be felt today with the dogma and doctrine of the church and seen in the faith expression of women who continue to be held hostage to the fear of being labeled a heretic. When it comes to how European women raise their sons and love the men in their lives, they are emotionally detached for fear of being seen as women who have their own voice, value, and virtue. This independence threatens the hold that historical misogyny has had on religion and society.

The African American woman was subjected to an intentional annihilation of her personhood through systemic oppression due to her gender and race. She was strategically used to alter the intellectual, emotional, and spiritual future of African Americans. In a document said to be penned by Willie Lynch in 1712, the female was strategically used by slave masters to change the course of history:

Take the female and run a series of tests on her to see if she will submit to your desires willingly. Test her in every way, because she is the most important factor for good economics. If she shows any sign of resistance in submitting completely to your will, do not hesitate to use the bullwhip on her to extract that last bit of [b----] out of her. Take care not to kill her, for in doing so, you spoil good economics. When in complete submission, she will train her offsprings in the early years to submit to labor when they become of age. Understanding is the best thing. Therefore, we shall go deeper into this area of the subject matter concerning what we have produced here in this breaking process of the female nigger. We have reversed the relationship; in her natural uncivilized state, she would have a strong dependency on the uncivilized nigger male, and she would have a limited protective tendency toward her independent male offspring and would raise male offsprings to be dependent like her. Nature had provided for this type of balance. We reversed nature by burning and pulling a civilized nigger apart and bullwhipping the other to the point of death, all in her presence. By her being left alone, unprotected, with the male image destroyed, the ordeal caused her to move from her psychologically dependent state to a frozen, independent state. In this frozen, psychological state of independence, she will raise her male and female offspring in reversed roles. For fear of the young male's life, she will psychologically train him to be mentally weak and dependent, but physically strong. Because she has become psychologically independent, she will train her female offsprings to be psychologically independent. What have you got? You've got the nigger woman out front and the nigger man behind and scared. This is a perfect situation of sound sleep and economics. Before the breaking process, we had to be alertly on guard at all times. Now, we can sleep soundly, for out of frozen fear his woman stands guard for us. He cannot get past her early slave-molding process. He is a good tool, now ready to be tied to the horse at a tender age. By the time a nigger boy reaches the age of sixteen, he is soundly broken in and ready for a long life of sound and efficient work and the reproduction of a unit of good labor force. Continually through the breaking of uncivilized savage niggers, by throwing the nigger female savage into a frozen psychological state of independence, by killing the protective male image, and by creating a submissive dependent mind of the nigger male slave, we have created an orbiting cycle that turns on its own axis forever, unless a phenomenon occurs and re-shifts the position of the male and female slave. We breed two nigger males with two nigger females. Then, we take the nigger male away from them and keep them moving and working. Say one nigger female bears a nigger female and the other bears a nigger male; both nigger females—being without influence of the nigger male image, frozen with an independent psychology—will raise their offspring into reverse positions. The one with the female offspring will teach her to be like herself, independent and negotiable. The one with the nigger male offspring, she being frozen subconscious fear for his life, will raise him to be mentally dependent and weak, but physically strong; in other words, body over mind. Now, in a few years when these two offsprings become fertile for early reproduction, we will mate and breed them and continue the cycle.

While it may be true that the authentication of the document is questionable, the content of the document rings true on many levels. African American women have been conditioned to fear for the lives of the men in their lives. They have done whatever necessary to protect them during slavery and have taught their daughters to do the same. Generation after generation of women have held men as precious commodities that can be snatched away at any time. Our fear of loving him unconditionally and him being ripped away has caused an emotional detachment to embed itself in the way that we raise our sons and love the men in our lives. Over time we have transposed the fear of losing him to "Master" to fear of losing him period. African American women have stood the test of time when it comes to being strong, being innovative, and being a leader. All of these things have helped to shape who she is and it has also made her a target as men struggle to reclaim the manhood that was ripped away from them. Let's Make A Slave fostered mistrust, miscommunication, and misappropriation of faith among women and men who were at one time on the same side of the truth. The truth has always been that we are all created in the image and likeness of God with voice, value, and virtue.

What do the Malleus Maleficarum and Let's Make A Slave have to do with Spiritual Alpha Females? Both documents stand as measuring sticks to how women have been perceived and portrayed spiritually and intellectually. Neither document gave women a voice, neither document gave women value, and neither document gave women virtue. As women have evolved in their understanding of themselves, their self-perception has been jaded by the misrepresentation and misappropriation of the fore mentioned documents. European American women hated African American women because the white men who owned them had sex with them. Their men told them that they were enticed by the slave women instead of telling the truth that they were intrigued by them. Instead of blaming their husbands, they internalized the lie that black women were seducers who enticed their men. African American women hated white women for not honoring the sisterhood and protecting them from their husbands. Women have been held hostage to the lie of who they have been told that they are and it has hindered their ability to walk in the fullness of who *They* created them to be. The movement from Alpha Female to Spiritual Alpha Female would have moved a lot faster if women were given the grace and the space to stand in the fullness of who they are. Unfortunately, the historical misogyny that is embedded in the fabric of religion has slowed down the movement but not stopped it completely. Over time, many other publications including the King James Version of the Bible prescribed language and imagery of women in a negative light. Darwin played a pivotal role in how women are perceived and presented spiritually and intellectually. Darwin finished his first discourse on evolution in 1859. He infused the female inferiority doctrine into biology and theology. Bergman (1992) taught that the differences between men and women were due partly, or even largely, to sexual selection. A male must prove himself physically and intellectually superior to other males in the competition for females to pass his genes on, whereas a woman must only be superior in sexual attraction. Darwin also concluded that 'sexual selection depended on two different intraspecific activities; the male struggle with males for possession of females; and female choice of a mate. Evolution depended on a struggle of individuals of one sex, generally male, for the possession of the other sex. According to Rosser (1992) the Darwinian concept of male superiority served to increase the secularization of society, and made more palatable the acceptance of the evolutionary naturalist view that humans were created by natural law rather than divine direction.

As I began to look at some misogynistic texts in the Bible, I could see how the effects of the horrors of the Malleus Maleficarum, Let's Make a Slave, and Darwinism have remained today. According to Rhodes (1987) a feminist analysis of the Christian Church's attitude toward women concludes that the churches have perpetuated a fear and hatred of women most powerfully expressed in their attitudes toward sexuality. The negative attitude stems from a dualistic view of life and of the sexes. Woman is associated with the body, feelings, and sexuality; man with the mind, spirit, and rationality. In this view, the mind is superior and should control the body. Spirituality transcends nature and is therefore superior to our bodily (animal) nature. The evidence of that is found in many of the stories of women in the Bible, such as Jezebel, who has been called harlot without substantial evidence to that affect. In the accounts of Jezebel (1 Kings 18:4, 13: 19:1-2: 21:1-16) we have a woman who is operating in her authority as Queen, although some scholars have added a sexual connotation to her character. I have not found anywhere in the text that shows Jezebel using her sexuality to get what she wants. I have not found anywhere in the text where you see Jezebel cheating on her husband with other men. I have not found anywhere in the text where you see Jezebel doing anything outside of her role as Queen. Although God holds her accountable for killing all the prophets that she did, it still does not justify changing a queen into a harlot. Jezebel was a foreign wife, and the patriarchal writers have written into the text that she was a sexually motivated choice for Ahab. Education about women in the Bible, enlightenment about who God has called them to be, and empowerment to walk in that calling all play a vital part in empowering women to find their reflection and embrace it in the biblical text. The truth of the word changes things. The truth allows us to see beyond the limited understanding that we have about God, others, and ourselves. The influence of the early church speaks to the influence that their writings also had on men and women.

Brenner (2000) talks about Queen Jezebel. She says there is no doubt that the biblical and later accounts distort her portrait for several reasons, among which we can list her monarchic power, deemed unfit in a woman; her reported devotion to Elijah and other prophets of YHWH; her education and legal know how (shown in the Naboth affair); and her foreign origin. Ultimately, the same passages that disclaim Jezebel as evil, "whoring," and immoral are witness to her power and the need to curb it. I am amazed at how Jezebel's image has been distorted and disappointed that so many of us have believed this lie. I asked myself how did Jezebel go from Queen to harlot? I found my answer in the story of Jezebel in Revelation 2:20. The woman named Jezebel in Revelation has been associated with the Jezebel in 1 Kings. Pippin (2000) says

Revelation reveals only one opinion of this prophet Jezebel. The reader does not hear her perspective. She may have been a teacher or preacher in the congregation with views different from those of the author of this text; though we cannot prove her historical existence we can explore the cultural implications of giving a powerful woman with differing opinions the name Jezebel. It is a way of dismissing and shaming her. Powerful women are often humiliated and disempowered in the biblical text through accusations of sexual promiscuity. Beginning with Eve, women have been blamed as temptress and seducers of men. As a foreign woman, Jezebel is doubly "other", bringing with her both dangerous religion and sexuality.

It seems to me that Jezebel has been robbed of her true identity and it is only through taking another look at the text through a liberated lens that she will be restored to her original glory.

Mary Magdalene is another woman in the Bible whose image has been distorted. Her name appears thirteen times in the entire New Testament. The thirteen times includes parallel passages, that is, her name shows up twice in a story in Matthew, and the same story is in Mark and Luke. Mary is never mentioned in the book of Acts, in the letters to Paul, or in any of the other writings of the New Testament. The Apostolic Fathers just after the New Testament and many of the earliest church fathers did not mention her either. During Jesus' entire public ministry, prior to his crucifixion, Mary is mentioned once, and that is only in Luke 8:2. Matthew, Mark, and John do not mention her at all prior to the crucifixion. There are 16 women named in the four gospels 6 are named Mary. The confusion about which Mary is which, adds to her distorted image. Mark 16:9 is where Jesus appeared to Mary Magdalene from whom he cast out seven demons. Mark 14:3-9 talks about an unnamed woman who anoints Jesus' head prior to his arrest and trial. Jesus praises her for anointing him for his burial. John 12:1-8 is the same story and the woman is named Mary. Luke 7:37-39 is similar to Mark except the woman is a sinner. In Mark they were in the house of Simon the Pharisee while in John they were in the house of Mary of Bethany. According to Ehrman (2006) when this third story is taken to refer to that same event as Mark's and John's, then what results is a garbled account, not found in Mark, John, or Luke, in which Jesus is anointed by a sinful woman named Mary. The category "sinner" then somehow gets translated to mean "prostitute" (which it didn't mean-it simply meant a woman who did not keep the law rigorously), with the result that Jesus is thought to have been anointed by a prostitute named Mary.

Scholars have concluded that this association was discovered to have its origin in year 591 CE, in a sermon delivered by none other than Pope Gregory the Great (540-604 CE):

She whom Luke calls the sinful woman, whom John calls Mary, we believe to be the Mary from whom seven devils were ejected according to Mark, And what did these seven devils signify, if not all the vices?...It is clear, brothers, that the woman previously used the unguent to perfume her flesh in forbidden acts. What she therefore displayed more scandalously, she was now offering to God in a more praiseworthy manner. She had coveted with earthly eyes, but now through penitence these are consumed with tears. She displayed her hair to set off her face, but now her hair dries her tears. She had spoken proud things with her mouth, but in kissing the Lord's feet, she now planted her mouth on the Redeemer's feet. For every delight, therefore, she had had in herself, she now immolated herself. She turned the mass of her crimes to virtues, in order to serve God entirely in penance, for as much as she had wrongly held God in contempt.

This sermon served as the foundation for Mary Magdalene going from a disciple to a prostitute. Myers (2000) says:

The later traditions about Mary Magdalene developed in two directions. The earlier tradition, which has prevailed more strongly in the East, concerns her stature as discloser of special revelations from Jesus, as shown in a number of non-canonical Gnostic works. *The Gospel of Phillip* interprets the presence of the three Marys in John's crucifixion scene as an expression of their faithful and exemplary discipleship: the three Marys (Jesus' mother, aunt, and Mary Magdalene, his companion) "always walked with the Lord." The *Gospel of Peter* repeats the synoptic scene. Mary-who is here specifically, called a disciple (*mathetria*) of Jesus- again leads a group of women, of which she is the only one named. *The Dialogue of the Savior* features three partners in conversation with Jesus: Matthew, Mary, and Judas (not the betrayer, but the other member of the twelve by name). Which Mary is never specified, but in light of the many Gnostic dialogues in which Mary Magdalene plays a key role, it is surely she. Here she is called "a woman who had understood completely." In the *Pistis Sophia*, Mary Magdalene is again a major speaker, and she and John "the virgin" are said by Jesus to be the greatest of disciples."

Even Christ's acknowledgement of the importance of Magdalene's role couldn't save her from the patriarchal and cultural forces that would marginalize women. Schaberg (2003) argues that once the pro-Petrine tendencies in the Gospel of Luke were adopted by church leaders who wanted to diminish women's leadership roles and, as they "attach female sexuality to notions of evil, repentance and mercy," political and ideological forces superseded historical realities."

Earlier I talked about the tree analogy in which the female trees wrestled with the split-second decision to shrink back in the face of a male dominated tree society. In the analogy the truth about the equal creation was evident however the misinterpretation of the truth caused a chain of events that caused female trees to fear for their lives and do what they needed to do to survive. Today, women fear for their emotional and spiritual lives and do what they need to do to survive. Women have taken the helm of various denominations, have pushed past the foolishness of religiosity to rise in leadership, and have reclaimed the voice, value, and virtue of who they are created to be, however there are women who are still being held hostage to a patriarchal systemic oppression that quenches their spirit and causes them to shrink back into the fakeness of who they are to survive. The distortion of women like Queen Jezebel and

Jesus' disciple, Mary Magdalene, reinforce what Jeremiah 8 says about the scribes knowingly writing lies. Those lies that Jeremiah talks about have changed the course of history. According to Rogers (1966) the foundations of early Christian misogyny—its guilt about sex, its insistence on female subjection, its dread of female seduction—are all in St. Paul's epistles. They provided a convenient supply of divinely inspired misogynistic texts for any Christian writer who chose to use them; his statements on female subjection were still being quoted in the twentieth century opponents of equality for women. Misogyny is still running rampant today and has been spiritually aligned with God's plan for women. It continues to blow my mind that the religious community sanctions and glorifies sexism with God's stamp of approval. If I went into the workforce and they marginalized me because I am a woman, someone would be fired. In the church it is stamped with "holy approval". What do we do with that? Shrinking back is our way of protecting ourselves like the trees who held back from extending their branches.

Spiritual Injury

The current male centered biblical presentation of womanhood has altered self-perception, self-assurance, and self-confidence in many women to the point where they have been subjected to spiritual injury. Chaplain Doll (2017) defines spiritual injury as:

A conflict we face between what one believes to be true of God and what the Scriptures teach to be true of God. It is how one expresses their understanding of God and the Scriptures compared to what one experiences or perceives to be true of God. What one believes is true of God, is going against what one is experiencing, thus causing a conflict between one's beliefs and one's reality. Spiritual injuries are personal injuries and are unique to each person based upon their understanding of God, the Scripture, religious doctrine, and traditions. What may be a significant spiritual contradiction for one person may not be a spiritual contradiction for another, i.e., killing is always wrong vs. killing in war is permissible. It must be remembered that another person's lack of spiritual injury in one area does not invalidate the spiritual injury of another person. Our spiritual injuries are not based on someone else's religious belief or faith; it is based upon our own personal knowledge and faith in God. Recovering from spiritual injury begins when we confront the spiritual contradictions that have caused the injury.

The spiritual injury that some women have has been masked by compliance, minimization of self, and hiding. Unfortunately, women wrestle with what to do with embracing a presentation of God that says femaleness is less than.

Every woman finds herself along a spectrum of spiritual awakening in her journey out of her spiritual injury. Some women choose to stay in the quietness of their compliance and never challenge the exclusively male presentation of God. Some women minimize their femaleness in an effort to embrace the maleness that can never be fully their own Some women hide their disgust with the exclusively male presentation of God to protect themselves. A good example of all three is when women use male language to describe their God-given journey such as "spirit man". The spirit of God is gender neutral until it rests in a host. The gender of the host matters. *They* are the fullness of female and male in one. When the spirit rests in a man it is male. When the spirit rests in a woman it is female. The trauma comes when women are demonized for celebrating the Divine female image of God. Heaven forbid that we would use *She* for God. For more reasons than this book can explain, the maleness of God is held as sacred and anything contrary to that is seen as heresy, contrary to God. Spiritual injury has hindered our growth as women. We have suffered from spiritual trauma that has put gaps in our journey. Gaps are chasms in life where healing from life's trauma should be. The chasms do not allow us to grow. It is only when we embrace our own spiritual awakening that we will be able to bridge the intellectual, emotional, and spiritual gaps that present themselves. Cognitive dissonance occurs as a result of the intellectual gap, emotional detachment occurs as a result of the emotional gap, and internal disconnection for external engagement occurs as a result of the spiritual gap.

The intellectual gap that women experience stems from their learned ability to behave in ways that their intellect is against. A woman who thinks that God is beyond the male gender and continues to use male language to conform to the norm embodies an

75

intellectual gap. Cognitive dissonance theory by Festinger (1957) says that people feel an uncomfortable feeling, or dissonance, when their attitudes conflict with their behaviors. People experience both negative affect and psychological discomfort when their behaviors are different from the attitudes they hold. If I believe God is inclusive of female and male yet I fear using female language, in my mind I must tell myself that *She* is a figment of my imagination. According to Festinger, I am uncomfortable, have a negative affect, and psychological discomfort because my thought process and my behavior do not line up. Aronson's (1969) new aspect of cognitive dissonance theory states that dissonance occurs when a behavior is inconsistent with a person's sense of self and the behavior is important to the self. To reduce dissonance, people try to justify themselves to maintain a good and stable self-concept. The intellectual gap that women experience is a major factor in their spiritual journey. The Bible says in Romans 12:2 (NASB) do not be conformed to this world, but be transformed by the renewing of your mind, so that you may prove what the will of God is, that which is good and acceptable and perfect. The transformation of a woman's mind is hindered by male language, imagery, doctrine, and dogma that tells her she is less than. It is hard to hold on to a truth internally when externally it is being ripped out of your spirit.

The emotional gap that exists in many women stems from their heart being broken by the constant disappointment they experience as they attempt to hold on to hope that things will change. Many women sit in the quietness of their hearts waiting for their opportunity to be presented and received in the fullness of being created in the image and likeness of God. It never ceases to amaze me that we can see marginalization clearly through racial discrimination yet we minimize the same thing when it comes to gender discrimination. On an emotional level, women go through a process of separating their emotional response to being minimized and marginalized because they have a womb. The emotional detachment that occurs in our emotional gap is real. It is very hard to authentically have good feelings when what you are presented with breaks your heart. How can I really love a man who sees me as less than and treats me as such? How can I be emotionally attached to a God that is presented to me as my Creator yet also the One who sees me as less than? Emotional detachment refers to an inability to connect with others on an emotional level, as well as a means of coping with anxiety by avoiding certain situations that trigger it; it is often described as "emotional numbing" or dissociation. I often wonder why there is such a disconnection in the church when it comes to emotions. So often we are taught that our emotions are out of control and therefore should never be trusted. The tragedy is that we miss our healing on many levels when we deny the very nature of who we are. Jeremiah 8: 21-22 (KJV) God says, "For the hurt of the daughter of my people I am hurt. I am mourning; Astonishment has taken hold of me. *Is there* no balm in Gilead, *Is there* no physician there? Why then is there no recovery for the health of the daughter of my people?" As we look at this text we see that God shares God's emotions. So what does that mean for us? We are created in the image and likeness of God and if God talks about it then so should we.

The spiritual gap that exacerbates a woman's journey serves as the deciding factor in her movement toward God or away from God. Unfortunately, many women experience an internal disconnection from who they believe God is to engage externally with the lie of who God is presented to be. Women have wrestled to find their reflection within the partial fullness of God (exclusive maleness). They have had to disengage from their internal truth of their Divinely appointed reflection of the female fullness of *They* to externally engage in a world that eliminates their Divine female reflection and forces them to transpose the Divine reflection of maleness as their own. The movement from rejecting the Divine reflection of the fullness of femaleness to transposing the Divine reflection of partialness of maleness has not worked. The spiritual injury must be healed. Spiritually injured women have a struggle with managing their primary and secondary emotions. The secondary emotion is what is presented to others while the primary emotion is what is deep under the surface. Primary emotions are the ones that we feel first as we respond to situations. The secondary emotion only rises when the primary emotion is not given space to be expressed and dealt with. Our response to our emotions are primary and secondary as well. Our secondary response is what we show to others while our primary response is truly what lies beneath.

They is a cycle that women experience that can bring healing or hinder their healing. The spiritually injured woman cycle shows the primary emotion and response below and the secondary emotion and response above.

Spiritually Injured Woman Cycle

Secondary Response:
External Connection
Unhealthy, limited, masked

Secondary Emotion:
Spiritual Frustration

Primary Response:
Broken, Painful, Aggressive,
Guarded

Primary Emotion
Sadness, Seperated
Unimportant

The wrestle with the primary and secondary emotion and response can be likened to an iceberg. What you see on the surface is not the full picture of what you will encounter if you get close enough. As we look at the cycle, the spiritual injury causes a women's primary emotion of sadness and separation to be overshadowed by a secondary emotion of anger. She is spiritually frustrated on the surface with feeling unimportant underneath. Her secondary response is what we see on the outside while her primary response is what we don't readily see yet is manifested in the real meaning behind her behavior. The spiritually injured woman's primary response is to disconnect internally due to her brokenness and pain which causes her to be guarded. What she shows people is an external connection that is unhealthy and masked with a limited connection to God, herself, and others. An example of this would be a woman being told that she is anointed by God in Joel 2:28-29 (NKJV), "I will pour out My Spirit on all flesh; Your sons and your daughters shall prophesy, Your old men shall dream dreams, Your young men shall see visions. And also on my menservants and on my maidservants I will pour out my Spirit in those days." yet prohibited from walking in her anointing due to 1 Corinthians 14:34-35 (NKJV), "Let your women keep silent in the churches, for they are not permitted to speak; but they are to be submissive, as the law also says. And if they want to learn something, let them ask their own husbands at home; for it is shameful for women to speak in church." We move from being spiritually injured to being spiritually empowered as we allow the healing work of the truth about who God is and who we are to God to set us free from the lies that we have believed.

Spiritually Empowered Woman Cycle

Secondary Response:
Healthy, Authentic,
Loving

Secondary Emotion:
Happiness
Contentment

Primary Response:
Internal Connection
Secure

Primary Emotion
Love, Joy, Safe

The spiritually empowered woman, the spiritual alpha female, has the freedom to rest in her primary emotion and response. She has no need to move to a dysfunctional secondary because she is fully present with and for herself. This woman is happy and content because she feels loved and safe. Her external connection is healthy, authentic, and loving because she has no need to disconnect internally.

No matter what cycle a woman finds herself, healing is a major factor. The inner dysfunctional voice takes over in the spiritually injured woman when the primary emotion is not given a voice. Inevitably, the inner empowering voice shifts to the inner dysfunctional voice. The shift happens so subtly that shrinking happens in the blink of an eye whether the woman wants to or not. The primary emotion of the spiritually injured woman comes up against sanctioned sexism. The very soul of a woman is violated every time she is forced to embrace a God who is presented to her that rejects her because she is female. The spiritual core of who she is must then wrestle with her origin, her existence, and her destiny. How can a woman fully be present within herself if she constantly has to reconcile being rejected by a presented God who she desperately wants to love and be loved by? Spiritual injury is real in the lives of women from all walks of life. Unfortunately, sexism is embedded in the fabric of the Christian faith. It has tainted the presentation, the explanation, as well as the education around who God is to us and who we are to God. For many religions sexism is sanctioned through their education as well as their practice. Spiritual injury is inevitable yet never identified, recognized, or healed. The inner dysfunctional voice tells the spiritually injured woman that she has no right to her truth and who she is is not hers to decide. The church teaches that women are subject to male truth. Male truth about God has been presented and received as sacred. As women began to refute the sacred association of the male truth, they are portrayed as rebellious, lovers of themselves, and followers of Satan. The presentation of the Bible required quiet submission to a truth that minimized and marginalized women. God's true intent (love) for women was buried in the maleness of language and imagery. The truth is that God created women with reason and purpose. Who she was created to be and do has been changed to accommodate the male-centered version of a lie that has been presented as sacred truth. What women have experienced in response to the lie has been traumatic. The Spiritual Alpha Female has been empowered through engaging the biblical text through the lens of a liberated understanding of who God is and who she is in God. She walks in the fullness of who she is and does her best to help other women do the same. There is no shrinking for the Spiritual Alpha Female. She knows that she knows that she knows that she was created in the image and likeness of the Divine which is inclusive of female and male. There are two cycles that women experience as they move from hurt to healed: The Re-visitation of the Hurting Place and the Re-visitation of the Healing Place

The Re-visitation of the Hurting Place

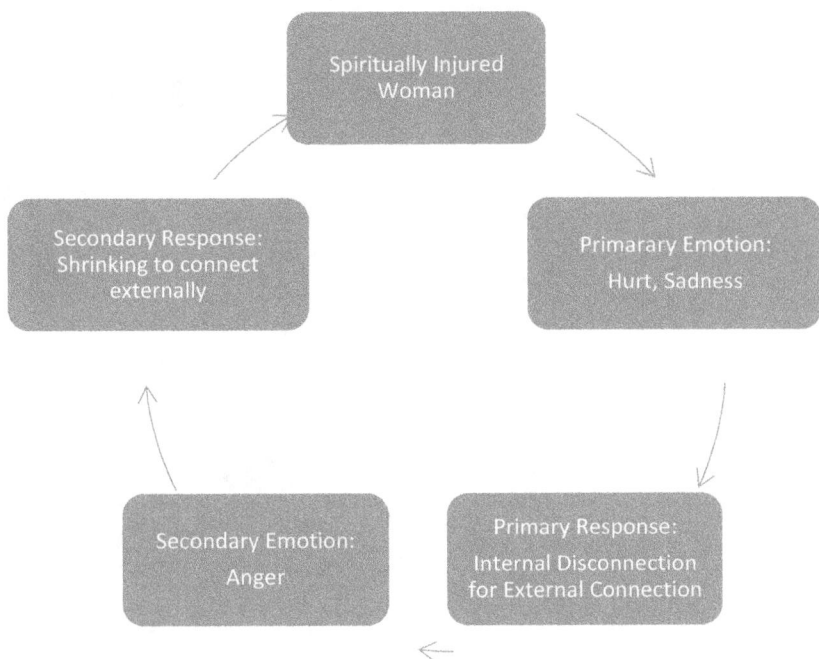

The Re-visitation of the Healing Place

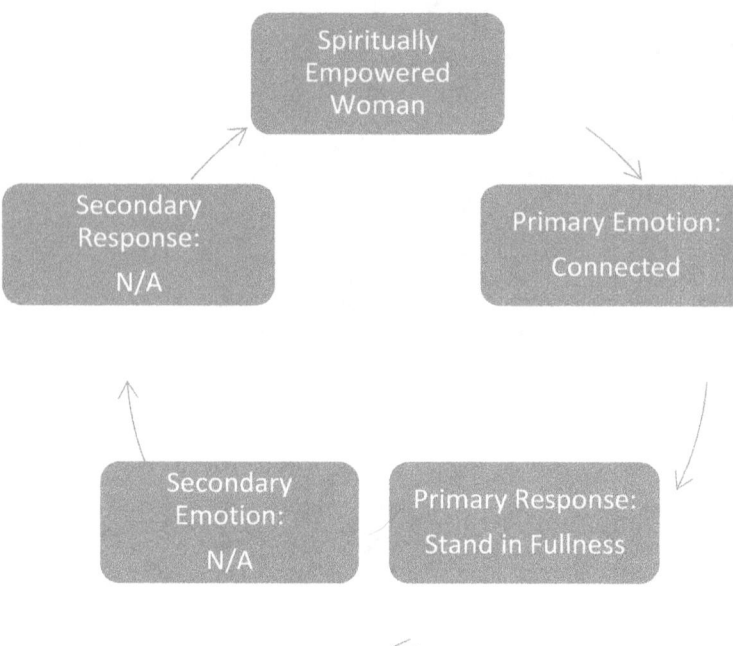

The two charts show a cyclical pattern that women live and relive every day. In one instance they are stuck and in the other they are free. The cycle of stuckness and the cycle of freedom can be a subtle difference; A word, a phrase, a gesture, a prayer, a new outlook on life. Spiritually injured women experience what I call the cyclical re-visitation of the hurting place and spiritually empowered women experience the cyclical re-visitation of the healing place. The re-visitation of the hurting place keeps the woman in a place of brokenness. We can find this experienced place in Jeremiah 8:8-22 (NLT)

How can you say, 'We are wise, and the law of the LORD is with us'? But behold, the lying pen of the scribes has made *it* into a lie. "The wise men are put to shame, they are dismayed and caught; Behold, they have rejected the word of the LORD, and what kind of wisdom do they have? "Therefore I will give their wives to others, their fields to new owners; Because from the least even to the greatest Everyone is greedy for gain; From the prophet even to the priest Everyone practices deceit. "They heal the brokenness of the daughter of My people superficially, Saying, 'Peace, peace,' But there is no peace. "Were they ashamed because of the abomination they had done? They certainly were not ashamed, And they did not know how to blush; Therefore they shall fall among those who fall; At the time of their punishment they shall be brought down," Says the LORD. "I will surely snatch them away," declares the LORD; "There will be no grapes on the vine and no figs on the fig tree, And the leaf will wither; And what I have given them will pass away. Why are we sitting still? Assemble yourselves, and let us go into the fortified cities and let us perish there, because the LORD our God has doomed us And given us poisoned water to drink, For we have sinned against the LORD. *We* waited for peace, but no good *came*; For a time of healing, but behold, terror! From Dan is heard the snorting of his horses; At the sound of the neighing of his stallions The whole land quakes; For they come and devour the land and its fullness, The city and its inhabitants. "For behold, I am sending serpents against you, Adders, for which there is no charm, and they will bite you," declares the LORD. My sorrow is beyond healing, My heart is faint *within me*! Behold, listen! The cry of the daughter of my people from a distant land: "Is the Lord not in Zion? Is her King not within her?" "Why have they provoked Me with their graven images, with foreign idols?" "Harvest is past, summer is ended, and we are not saved." For the brokenness of the daughter of my people I am broken; I mourn, dismay has taken hold of me. Is there no balm in Gilead? Is there no physician there?

- -

Why then has not the health of the daughter of my people been restored?

The cyclical re-visitation of the healing place is where restoration of the soul occurs. We can find this healing experience in Isaiah 52:1-3 (NLT):

> Wake up, wake up, O Zion! Clothe yourself with strength. Put on your beautiful clothes, O holy city of Jerusalem, for unclean and godless people will enter your gates no longer. Rise from the dust, O Jerusalem. Sit in a place of honor. Remove the chains of slavery from your neck, O captive daughter of Zion. For this is what the LORD says: "When I sold you into exile, I received no payment. Now I can redeem you without having to pay for you.

Jeremiah 8 is where we find the basis for the spiritually injured woman's move from her primary emotion to her secondary emotion. Her inner empowering voice shifts to her inner dysfunctional voice. Women are precious to God. Who we are, why we were created, and the footprint that we leave in this human experience is priceless. As we live, move, and have our being, the essence of our Spiritwoman is constantly being challenged by the misinterpretation and misrepresentation of God and God's word. Jeremiah 8 talks about God's displeasure with the hurt that has come from the scribes, Prophet, even the Priest to the *Daughter of my people*. The scribe has written words that hold women hostage to things that they have not even released through the shed blood of Christ. What the scribe says happened in the Garden, woman caused man to fall, is prescriptive beyond God sending Jesus Christ to restore humanity back to good standing with God. The first female/male relationship was not hierarchical. They were on a level playing field, they both heard the Garden rules, they both decided to be disobedient, yet she is punished for life and he is elevated. The Priest and the Prophet reinforce this misogynistic explanation and presentation of women and in Jeremiah 8 God is grieving the brokenness that they experience. God is holding men accountable for *healing the brokenness of the daughter of my people superficially*. (v. 11) Who we are and what God has called us to do is wrapped up in who God is, not who other people say God is. My Beloved Sisters, God is restoring our Spiritwoman. God is restoring our self-reflection and our self-identity. We have been spiritually injured by all the "isms" that have come to rob us of our true reflection and identity. God is restoring spiritual empowerment to you. So often we look externally to complete us internally. Today, God says I am restoring your brokenness which in turn will make you a spiritually empowered resource for other women who are broken. Isaiah 52 is where we find the basis for the spiritually empowered woman who has no need to shift from her primary emotion to a secondary emotion. The cycle will continue as long as women either stay in the dark or refuse the truth in the light. The bottom line is women in some parts of the world have a choice. In other parts of the world, women are far more marginalized and have no voice, rights, or access to empowerment. Regardless of the level of marginalization, the internal struggle for women is real.

Spiritual Awakening

How do we move from spiritual injury to spiritual awakening? Beloved, we heal as we talk about our experience. Difficult conversations occupy a separate space in our lives. We do not nor could we live entirely in this realm. They require much more energy than everyday conversation because they carry multiple levels of meaning that go well below the word we speak, the conversation speaks to the core of our identity. It gets so easy to push hard topics to the side and act like they do not matter. For the Spiritual Alpha Female, words heal and words cause brokenness. I am fully persuaded that constructive dialogue is the key to successful relationships among women who desire to stand in the fullness of who they are while helping other women do the same. It is strategic that women are discouraged from collaborating with other women. It is in the dismantling of the lie that women cannot work together where we find space for true Spiritual Alpha Females to take their rightful place in leadership. Wonder woman has been my absolute favorite character ever since I saw her on TV in the person of Linda Carter in the 70's. She was a majestic, powerful, beautiful, super smart woman and she came from a majestic, powerful, beautiful, super smart community of women. Her official title is Princess Diana of Themyscira, Daughter of Hippolyta. She was designed to empower women. According to Marston (1943), Wonder Woman's creator:

Not even girls want to be girls so long as our feminine archetype lacks force, strength, and power. Not wanting to be girls, they don't want to be tender, submissive, peace-loving as good women are. Women's strong qualities have become despised because of their weakness. The obvious remedy is to create a feminine character with all the strength of Superman plus all the allure of a good and beautiful woman.

My affinity to Wonder Woman was for that very reason. I believed that I was able to be whoever I wanted and that did not include docility, domestication, and silence. Wonder Woman was everything I saw in me, powerful, beautiful, intelligent, and amazing. Over the course of many years there were attempts to sexualize her, minimize her, and make her less than her counterparts. She was created to be equal to Superman and Batman. She was powerful in her own right coming from a place with other women who were powerful in their own right. Wonder Woman is an excellent example of an alpha female leader yet I needed to find an alpha female leader who exemplified the spiritual grounding that I could model my life after. Proverbs 31 was my landing place.

This woman encompasses leadership on so many levels. There is so much that we can learn from her leadership characteristics. When I think about the fact that she is a portrait of a woman and not an actual woman I am encouraged and not intimidated by the expectation to be all of who she is. The portrait of this woman in Proverbs 31 reads this way:

The Contemporary English Version

These are the sayings that King Lemuel of Massa was taught by his mother. [2] My son Lemuel, you were born in answer to my prayers, so listen carefully. [3] Don't waste your life chasing after women! This has ruined many kings. [4] Kings and leaders should not get drunk or even want to drink. [5] Drinking makes you forget your responsibilities, and you mistreat the poor. [6] Beer and wine are only for the dying or for those who have lost all hope. [7] Let them drink and forget how poor and miserable they feel. [8] But you must defend those who are helpless and have no hope. [9] Be fair and give justice to the poor and homeless. In Praise of a Good Wife [10] A truly good wife is the most precious treasure a man can find! [11] Her husband depends on her, and she never lets him down. ¹² She is good to him every day of her life, ¹³ and with her own hands she gladly makes clothes. ¹⁴ She is like a sailing ship that brings food from across the sea. ¹⁵ She gets up before daylight to prepare food for her family and for her servants. ¹⁶ She knows how to buy land and how to plant a vineyard, ¹⁷ and she always works hard. ¹⁸ She knows when to buy or sell, and she stays busy until late at night. ¹⁹ She spins her own cloth, ²⁰ and she helps the poor and the needy. ²¹ Her family has warm clothing, and so she doesn't worry when it snows. ²² She does her own sewing, and everything she wears is beautiful. ²³ Her husband is a well-known and respected leader in the city. ²⁴ She makes clothes to sell to the shop owners. ²⁵ She is strong and graceful, as well as cheerful about the future. ²⁶ Her words are sensible, and her advice is thoughtful. ²⁷ She takes good care of her family and is never lazy. ²⁸ Her children praise her, and with great pride her husband says, ²⁹ "There are many good women, but you are the best!" ³⁰ Charm can be deceiving, and beauty fades away, but a woman who honors the LORD deserves to be praised.

[31] Show her respect—praise her in public for what she has done.

The Hebrew words used to describe this woman is *Eshet Chayil* "a woman of valor". The Hebrew word *eshet* is the construct of *isha* and *chayil* connotes bravery (Ps 76:6) capability (Prov 12:4) triumph (Ps 118:15) rampart (Ps 84:8) and wealth (Prov 13:22) The word is defined as strength, army, valiant, able, and excellence when it is making reference to men. The same word is defined as virtuous in the King James Version and good in the Contemporary English Version when it is making reference to women.

Chayil appears two times in reference to women: Ruth 3:11 and Proverbs 31:10 where it uses virtuous. When it makes reference to men they are strong, valiant, and able, why do they use virtuous for women? Virtuous comes with the connotation of being chaste, quiet in spirit, modest, and docile. Clearly this woman was strong, valiant, and able like any man. I believe that she was a powerful woman in her own right even though she is portrayed as one who is who she is based on her husband and children. We all have been taught a way of perceiving Proverbs 31. She is a woman who does what she does to please her husband, her children, and her God. I am suggesting that she is a collage of a woman who is who she is and does what she does because she is a Spiritual Alpha Female in her own strength. Her choice to be good to her husband and children does not define who she is. She defines who she is. This movement to *choose to be* instead of *being told to be* will be a challenge for some women. The whole idea of being considered rebellious when we question the male-centered and male-driven language, imagery, and system leaves some women frozen in their current state of spiritual injury. There is a sense of uncertainty as we learn a new way. What will people say? How will my new understanding affect my current reality? Who will I become as I walk this new path? Am I really ready to learn something that will change everything? Learning is a process. You will inevitably change over time, not all at once. According to Heifetz (1994):

> Not only can we learn, but we can manage our learning. Many societies in human history have died rather than adapt. Clarifying aspirations, facing problems, and developing a set of socially adaptive responses is not easy. Just as individuals resist the pain and dislocation that comes with changing their

attitudes and habits of behavior, societies resist learning as well. For a social system to learn, old patterns of relationship-balance of power, customary operating procedures, distributions of wealth-may be threatened. Old skills may be rendered useless. Beliefs, identity, and orienting values-images of justice, community, and responsibility-may be called into question. Humans can learn and cultures can change, but how much and how fast? Beloved, it is time. Change is here. Jeremiah 8 tells us that God is mourning because of our brokenness. Isaiah 52 tells us to loose the chains around our neck. The lie that we have been told about who we are and who we are to God is the chain which has caused our brokenness.

It is time for us to speak our own truth about how we live, move, and have our being. Like the Spiritual Alpha Female that is described in Proverbs 31, my voice and my value is unleashed on my terms. Meghan, Duchess of Sussex (2018) says it this way:

You realize that once you have access or a voice that people are willing to listen to, with that comes a lot of responsibility. Women don't need to find a voice, they have a voice. They need to feel empowered to use it and people need to be encouraged to listen. Yes you can have questions of self-doubt, and that's going to come up, that's human. But at the end of the day, you are enough exactly as you are. No matter what you look like, you should be taken seriously. And I think it is very important for me, also I think it's really great to be able to be a feminist and be feminine, to embrace both. And if we treat ourself like our own best friends, I think that it's like having the best cheerleader ever with you.

My sister, it is time to be your own best cheerleader. In the coming pages, we will unleash leadership principles from Proverbs 31 through 8 Spiritual Alpha Females: Queen Sheba, a confident woman with authentic leadership through the lens of verse 10; Queen Michal, a loving woman with emotional intelligent leadership through the lens of verses 11-12, and 23; Queen Vashti, an innovative woman with transformational leadership through the lens of verses 13-16, 18-19, 21-22, and 24; Queen Bathsheba, a wise woman with primal leadership through the lens of verses 17, and 25-26; Queen Abigail, a kind woman with path-goal leadership through the lens of verse 20; Queen Esther, a surrendered woman with servant leadership through the lens of verses 27-28; Prophet Miriam, a powerful woman with situational leadership through the lens of verse 29; Prophet Deborah, a woman of great faith with steward leadership through the lens of verse 30; and You, a woman who honors God with the fullness of who you are through the lens of verse 31.

Now what? Now Who? Now When? Now How? The next step is the space and place that only you can decide. Some of us can jump up and change everything right away, some of us need to take some time to strategically bring about change, and some of us will remain right where we are and give space and grace for other women to take the torch further. 2 Kings 7:3-4b (KJV) answers my questions and maybe it will answer yours as well. It says, "And there were four leprous men at the entering of the gate: and they said one to another, why sit we here until we die? If we say, we will enter into the city, then the famine is in the city, and we shall die there: and if we sit still here, we die also." You might be wondering what this story has to do with being a Spiritual Alpha Female. In the story, four men had been marginalized, minimized, and over looked because of what society says about their state of being. They were leprous and that meant they were unclean and not welcomed. Women have been marginalized, minimized, and over looked because of what the church and society says about their state of being. We have a womb and that means we are unclean and not welcomed. In the Bible lepers are put out of the camp while women have been forced to live among the people experiencing the horror of being treated as unclean and unwelcomed.

The lepers asked a pivotal question, "Why sit here until we die?" It seems to me that they came to a place in life where they said enough is enough with being held hostage to other people's beliefs and decisions. Other people dictated their value and their voice. Women find themselves in the same space. Granted there are denominations that are liberated and women have equal access to all that God has to offer. Unfortunately, sexism is embedded in the fabric of faith and society. Women may be liberated in one arena yet still held hostage to male language, imagery, and systems. Like the lepers, I have decided that enough is enough with being held hostage to male beliefs and decisions about who I am and who I am to God. I, like the lepers, have decided that dying is possible yet I refuse to not try to live. I'm making the choice to live my truth through the lenses of my understanding of who God is to me and who I am to God. God has given me value and voice. The Proverbs 31 collage of a woman has liberated me and allowed me to see that the Spiritual Alpha Female is a collage of a woman. I have the ability to choose. If I choose to be a mother, so be it, If I choose to be a wife, so be it. If I choose to be a housewife, so be it. If I choose to be a business mogul, so be it. If I choose to be both, so be it. I can lead, follow, cook, clean, mentor, coach, build, buy and sell, and so much more. The bottom line is, I choose what works for me. "She whom the Son has set free, Is Free Indeed" I am a Spiritual Alpha Female, who are you?

Spiritual Position of Attention

I was blessed to go to a Women in Military Retreat that changed the course of my life. There were powerful women who came together to share their struggles and their joys as they walked their call in the military. One woman in particular shifted my thinking. Chaplain (Colonel) Janet Yarlott Horton US Army (Ret) was pivotal in the early days of integrating women into the military. She talked at length about how God continuously orchestrated her path to be in the right place at the right time for God to use her to be a trailblazer. One of the things that she talked about was how she was able to hear God's voice in the midst of the loud male voices that attempted to deny her access to leadership. She said that she would come to a spiritual position of attention. She would shut out everything that was not like God with the intention of getting in a place of "yes". She had to shut out the noise, the stress, the negativity, the pressures of life as a woman, and anything else that distracted her from saying yes to God. In this spiritual position of attention, she was able to find peace, rest, and her "yes". Spiritual

Position of Attention (SPA) is our call to find peace, rest, and our "yes". Amazingly, the (SPA) and the spa have a lot in common. You seek peace at the spa from the cares of your life, you seek rest at the spa as you try to escape your busy life, and you weed through the many "nos" that you get to find the place of "yes" to find meaning and purpose in your life. Look at the spa as your natural retreat and the SPA as your spiritual retreat. The spiritual SPA and the natural spa draw you in. The natural meets your physical needs and the spiritual meets your physical, emotional and intellectual needs. God is your foundation, faith is your framework, and leadership is your future. It is time to spend more of your energy focusing on your spiritual need for the SPA instead of your natural need for the spa. For the Spiritual Alpha Female, we come to the spiritual position of attention to show respect to God as God speaks to us. It is coming to a spiritual internal space where we turn to God with our whole heart and really listen to what God wants to reveal to us. Each chapter will lift a biblical text for you to consider your peace from God, your rest in God, and your "yes" to God.

Chapter Two

Principle #1

Upright Character

[10] Who can find a virtuous wife? For her worth is far above rubies.

The Spiritual Alpha Female is a woman who if fully present in herself with the understanding that God has gifted her and anointed her to be different. She is confident without being conceited, she is strong while being meek, and she is amazing in her own right. Principle #1 is upright character. Proverbs 31:10 shares that this woman's *worth is far above rubies*. Upright character is paramount because you must match your confidence in you with God's value of who you are. Your worth is reflected in how you value or devalue yourself. How you live, move, and have your being in confidence must be a mirror of how you honor God with who you are. No one will need to tell you how to behave, what to say, and where to go. Your love for God and your understanding of God's love for you will order your steps, guide your speech, and manage how you love. This principle will be illuminated through The Queen of Sheba. She is a confident woman who demonstrated authentic leadership.

The Lady: The Queen of Sheba

The Queen of Sheba is a woman who traveled a long way to experience the wisdom of King Solomon. Of the two queens in the Bible who are named as rulers, it is the Queen of Sheba we find written about most in the Scriptures. She appears in I Kings 10, 2 Chronicles 9, Matthew, and Luke:

1 Kings 10:1-13 (NASB)

Now when the queen of Sheba heard about the fame of Solomon concerning the name of the LORD, she came to test him with difficult questions. [2] So she came to Jerusalem with a very large retinue, with camels carrying spices and very much gold and precious stones. When she came to Solomon, she spoke with him about all that was in her heart.[3] Solomon answered all her questions; nothing was hidden from the king which he did not explain to her. [4] When the queen of Sheba perceived all the wisdom of Solomon, the house that he had built, [5] the food of his table, the seating of his servants, the attendance of his waiters and their attire, his cupbearers, and his stairway by which he went up to the house of the LORD, there was no more spirit in her. [6] Then she said to the king, "It was a true report which I heard in my own land about your words and your wisdom. [7] Nevertheless I did not believe the reports, until I came and my eyes had seen it. And behold, the half was not told me. You exceed *in* wisdom and prosperity the report which I heard. [8] How blessed are your men, how blessed are these your servants who stand before you continually *and* hear your wisdom. [9] Blessed be the LORD your God who delighted in you to set you on the throne of Israel; because the LORD loved Israel forever, therefore He made you king, to do justice and righteousness." [10] She gave the king a hundred and twenty talents of gold, and a very great *amount* of spices and precious stones. Never again did such abundance of spices come in as that which the queen of Sheba gave King Solomon. [11] Also the ships of Hiram, which brought gold from Ophir, brought in from Ophir a very great *number of* almug trees and precious stones. [12] The king made of the almug trees supports for the house of the LORD and for the king's house, also lyres and harps for the singers; such almug trees have not come in again nor have they been seen to this day. [13] King Solomon gave to the queen of Sheba all her desire which she requested, besides what he gave her according to his royal bounty. Then she turned and went to her own land together with her servants.

2 Chronicles 9

Now when the queen of Sheba heard of the fame of Solomon, she came to Jerusalem to test Solomon with difficult questions. She had a very large retinue, with camels carrying spices and a large amount of gold and precious stones; and when she came to Solomon, she spoke with him about all that was on her heart. Solomon answered all her questions; nothing was hidden from Solomon which he did not explain to her. [3] When the queen of Sheba had seen the wisdom of Solomon, the house which he had built, [4] the food at his table, the seating of his servants, the attendance of his ministers and their attire, his cupbearers and their attire, and his stairway by which he went up to the house of the LORD, she was breathless. [5] Then she said to the king, "It was a true report which I heard in my own land about your words and your wisdom. [6] Nevertheless I did not believe their reports until I

- - -

came and my eyes had seen it. And behold, the half of the greatness of your wisdom was not told me. You surpass the report that I heard. ⁷ How blessed are your men, how blessed are these your servants who stand before you continually and hear your wisdom. ⁸ Blessed be the LORD your God who delighted in you, setting you on His throne as king for the LORD your God; because your God loved Israel establishing them forever, therefore He made you king over them, to do justice and righteousness." ⁹ Then she gave the king one hundred and twenty talents of gold and a very great *amount of* spices and precious stones; there had never been spice like that which the queen of Sheba gave to King Solomon. ¹⁰ The servants of Huram and the servants of Solomon who brought gold from Ophir, also brought algum trees and precious stones. ¹¹ From the algum trees the king made steps for the house of the LORD and for the king's palace, and lyres and harps for the singers; and none like that was seen before in the land of Judah.¹² King Solomon gave to the queen of Sheba all her desire which she requested besides a return for what she had brought to the king. Then she turned and went to her own land with her servants.

Matthew 12:42

"The Queen of the South will rise up with this generation at the judgment and will condemn it, because she came from the ends of the earth to hear the wisdom of Solomon; and behold, something greater than Solomon is here.

Luke 11:31

The Queen of the South will rise up with the men of this generation at the judgment and condemn them, because she came from the ends of the earth to hear the wisdom of Solomon; and behold, something greater than Solomon is here.

The Queen of Sheba is never given a name in the Bible. What we do know is that she was already ruling where she came from. Unfortunately, the Bible does not give us a lot about her before she talked with King Solomon or after she talked with King Solomon. Her impact was significant enough for her to be mentioned in the New Testament. According to Jewish, Islamic, and Ethiopian tradition she had a son with King Solomon. Unlike many women in the Bible, this Queen speaks. She shared her heart with King Solomon and is given the opportunity to tell him how his wisdom has impacted her. I believe that her encounter with King Solomon enhanced her ability to lead in an authentic way.

Her Leadership: Authentic Leadership

Leadership has been defined in many ways. While the definitions vary, the basic premise of what leadership is remains consistent. Bass & Stogdill (1990) share that eadership is an interaction between two or more members of a group that often involves a structuring or restructuring of the situation and the perceptions and expectations of the members. Leaders are agents of change persons whose acts affect other people more than other people's acts affect them. Leadership occurs when one group member modifies the motivation or competencies of others in the group. Of the many definitions of leadership, one that I like the most places emphasis on followship. Northouse (2013) defines leadership as a process that is not a trait or characteristic that resides in the leader, but rather a transactional event that occurs between the leader and the followers. Leadership is nothing without followship. People choose to follow a leader for various reasons. According to

Rosenbach, Taylor, and Youndt, (2012) if we are to begin to understand what leadership is, it is worthwhile to examine what leadership is not. Leadership is not hierarchical, top down, or based on positional power and authority. True leadership has a sense of positivity that undergirds the flow of leadership. The Queen of Sheba had followers who honored her leadership. She was an authentic leader who understood the value of developing her own abilities. Authentic leadership emphasizes a leader who is self-aware, transparent, a balanced thinker, and ethical. The Queen demonstrated authentic leadership as she travelled to learn from King Solomon's wisdom. When it comes to authentic leadership, it is up to the leader to decide how they want to impact their followers. No matter how much you think you know about leadership, there is always more to learn.

Authentic leaders understand who they are to their followers and desire to be better leaders. Self-directed learning becomes their means of growth and development. According to Northouse (2013) the crux of leadership development that works is *self-directed learning*: intentionally developing or strengthening an aspect of who you are or who you want to be, or both. This requires first getting a strong image of your *ideal self,* as well as an accurate picture of your *real self* –who you are now. The Queen of Sheba looked to King Solomon to her help differentiate between her ideal self and her real self. She wanted to gain insight from King Solomon that ultimately helped to reshape who she was becoming. Self-directed learning helps leaders figure out those things that are true and those things that are not true about themselves. It also speaks to the necessity for leaders to be mentally, emotionally, and spiritually healthy.

Who I am and who I become is contingent upon my genetics, my environment, my examples, and my willingness to change. We see countless examples of people who start out one way and end up another. I remember a story of a man who was mean. His family did not like him, his employees did not like him, and pretty much no one liked him. He was impatient, intolerant, and unappreciative. One day his wife ran into a pastor and asked him to counsel her husband. She shared with the pastor that her husband was very wealthy and successful but no one liked him. One day that pastor called him and asked if they could talk one day. The man said sure and scheduled a visit with the Pastor. The pastor met the man at his beautiful house and they began to talk about his life. The man shared that he got everything he has on his own. He said that no one ever helped him and he has been alone his whole life. The pastor looked at him and said who fed you when you were a baby? The man looked at the pastor and said my mom. The pastor said who changed your diapers when you were a baby? The man said my mom. He said you sure have a big house how do you keep all of those toilets clean? He said I don't the cleaning service does. He said your children are beautiful it is amazing that you raised them all by yourself. He said my wife helps me raise them. Finally, the pastor said wow it seems like there have been many people who have helped you along the way and you pretty much have always had people do things for you. The man said that is true pastor. The pastor said you are hard on the people who are actually helping you. The man said you are right pastor and from that day forward he began to see the value that other people had and how they make his lavish life possible. The man became grateful, appreciative, and kind and people began to love the new person he became.

I tell that story because it speaks to the unconscious nature of humanity. That man was portraying the person that he thought he should be instead of the man he really could be. It took someone to open his eyes to the truth in order for him to change. I see value in self-directed learning as long as the learner understands that people along the self-directed path must be used to help the person see what they would not necessarily see on their own. Everyone has a contextual understanding of who they are and why they are the way that they are. Leadership is relative to the social construct, family dynamics, environment, and faith. No matter what we attempt to do or say, the truth is that every culture has their own way of doing things. The Queen of Sheba chose to talk with the wisest man alive and the impact of that had to change her leadership approach. She was walking down the path of self-directed learning and it changed her life for the better. I continue to believe that who you are and who you become is forever entangled in what you believe about yourself and what you believe about others

Authentic leaders pay particular attention to their use of power. Power and the use of power can make or break a leader. Northouse (2013) talks about the concept of power as it relates to leadership where he says, power is the capacity or potential to influence. People have power when they have the ability to affect others' beliefs, attitudes, and courses of action. Judges, doctors, pastors, coaches, and teachers are all examples of people who have the potential to influence us. When they do, they are using their power, the resource they draw on to effect change in us. There is nothing wrong with having power and influence unless you use it to marginalize people. Women have been conditioned to believe that they are not the bearers of their own power. Throughout the Bible we see stories of women who have no power. Whether that power was never given or taken, the woman is left questioning her faith and her future. The Queen of Sheba had power and chose to get wisdom from a person who also had power to help her use her power in a better way. Leadership comes with power in that you have the opportunity to influence your followers. It takes discipline as a leader to manage your use and possible misuse of your power.

Your Lesson: Be a Confident Woman

The Queen of Sheba left the comforts of her leadership to glean some wisdom from a wise King. She understood that learning is an ongoing and necessary process. As we learn and grow as leaders we must have a level of confidence in who God called us to be. Confidence in God is not the same as being conceited. Conceit is having unbalanced faith in yourself with no credit given to God. Confidence is having balanced faith in yourself with the understanding that the Spirit of God is standing tall inside of you to give you what you need to live, move, and have your being in God. The Spiritual Alpha Female walks in absolute confidence that she is equipped to be all that God called her to be. She values herself above rubies the same way that God does. In her confidence she understands that there are people who are sent to sow into her life to make her better. King Solomon sowed into the Queen of Sheba's life and made her better. Please understand that true learners seek teachers just like the Queen of Sheba. Your walk as a confident woman who leads is contextual to you. Get to know you, be authentic, be confident.

Spiritual Position of Attention

Enlightenment of a Leader

NEVER FORGET WHO YOU ARE

And blessed is she who believed that what was spoken to her by the Lord would be fulfilled." Luke 1:45 (NET)

Peace from God:_____
_____
_____
_____
_____

My rest in God:_____
_____
_____
_____
_____

My "yes" to God:_____
_____
_____
_____
_____
_____

Chapter Three

Principle #2
Name Your Truth

11 The heart of her husband safely trusts her; So he will have no lack of gain.12 She does him good and not evil all the days of her life. 23 Her husband is known in the gates when he sits among the elders of the land.

Every woman has to make her own choice about the man she loves. We choose how we love our men, or so we think. For some of us, we have been acculturated to place the love of the man ahead of our love for ourselves. That in and of itself is not bad if he loves you the same way. The problem comes in when we value him more than we are valued by him. There is a depth to a woman's love that men will never understand. When we love fully it is as if our love is rooted into the very core of our being to the point that we don't know where we begin and he ends. The amazing thing about that is this, when the love is reciprocal it is life changing. Verses 11, 12, and 23 describes the depth of the love that women carry for the men that they love and their response to that love. Queen Michal had that love for King David. Her story shares the lengths to which women go for love. Principle # 2 is Name Your Truth. This principle will be illuminated through Queen Michal. She is a loving woman who demonstrated emotional intelligent leadership.

The Lady: Queen Michal

Queen Michal was the youngest daughter of King Saul. She, unlike many women in the Bible, is said to have loved a man. Her story is told in 1 Samuel 14; 1 Samuel 18; 1 Sam 19; 1 Samuel 25; 2 Samuel 3; 2 Samuel 6; and 1 Chronicles 15.

1 Samuel 14:49

Saul's sons were Jonathan, Ishvi and Malki-Shua. The name of his older daughter was Merab, and that of the younger was Michal.

1 Samuel 18:20-28

[20] Now Saul's daughter Michal was in love with David, and when they told Saul about it, he was pleased. [21] "I will give her to him," he thought, "so that she may be a snare to him and so that the hand of the Philistines may be against him." So Saul said to David,

"Now you have a second opportunity to become my son-in-law."

²² Then Saul ordered his attendants: "Speak to David privately and say, 'Look, the king likes you, and his attendants all love you; now become his son-in-law.'" ²³ They repeated these words to David. But David said, "Do you think it is a small matter to become the king's son-in-law? I'm only a poor man and little known." ²⁴ When Saul's servants told him what David had said, ²⁵ Saul replied, "Say to David, 'The king wants no other price for the bride than a hundred Philistine foreskins, to take revenge on his enemies. Saul's plan was to have David fall by the hands of the Philistines. ²⁶ When the attendants told David these things, he was pleased to become the king's son-in-law. So before the allotted time elapsed, ²⁷ David took his men with him and went out and killed two hundred Philistines and brought back their foreskins. They counted out the full number to the king so that David might become the king's son-in-law. Then Saul gave him his daughter Michal in marriage. ²⁸ When Saul realized that the LORD was with David and that his daughter Michal loved David, ²⁹ Saul became still more afraid of him, and he remained his enemy the rest of his days.

1 Sam 19:11-17

[11] Saul sent men to David's house to watch it and to kill him in the morning. But Michal, David's wife, warned him, "If you don't run for your life tonight, tomorrow you'll be killed." [12] So Michal let David down through a window, and he fled and escaped. [13] Then Michal took an idol and laid it on the bed, covering it with a garment and putting some goats' hair at the head. [14] When Saul sent the men to capture David, Michal said, "He is ill." [15] Then Saul sent the men back to see David and told them, "Bring him up to me in his bed so that I may kill him." [16] But when the men entered, there was the idol in the bed, and at the head was some goats' hair. [17] Saul said to Michal, "Why did you deceive me like this and send my enemy away so that he escaped?" Michal told him, "He said to me, 'Let me get away. Why should I kill you?'"

1 Samuel 25:44

But Saul had given his daughter Michal, David's wife, to Paltiel son of Laish, who was from Gallim.

2 Samuel 3:13-14

[13] "Good," said David. "I will make an agreement with you. But I demand one thing of you: Do not come into my presence unless

you bring Michal daughter of Saul when you come to see me."

¹⁴ Then David sent messengers to Ish-Bosheth son of Saul, demanding, "Give me my wife Michal, whom I betrothed to myself for the price of a hundred Philistine foreskins." ¹⁵ So Ish-Bosheth gave orders and had her taken away from her husband Paltiel son of Laish. ¹⁶ Her husband, however, went with her, weeping behind her all the way to Bahurim. Then Abner said to him, "Go back home!" So he went back.

2 Samuel 6:16-23

² Now King David was told, "The LORD has blessed the household of Obed-Edom and everything he has, because of the ark of God." So David went to bring up the ark of God from the house of Obed-Edom to the City of David with rejoicing. ¹³ When those who were carrying the ark of the LORD had taken six steps, he sacrificed a bull and a fattened calf. ¹⁴ Wearing a linen ephod, David was dancing before the LORD with all his might, ¹⁵ while he and all Israel were bringing up the ark of the LORD with shouts and the sound of trumpets. ¹⁶ As the ark of the LORD was entering the City of David, Michal daughter of Saul watched from a window. And when she saw King David leaping and dancing before the LORD,

she despised him in her heart. ¹⁷ They brought the ark of the LORD and set it in its place inside the tent that David had pitched for it, and David sacrificed burnt offerings and fellowship offerings before the LORD. ¹⁸ After he had finished sacrificing the burnt offerings and fellowship offerings, he blessed the people in the name of the LORD Almighty. ¹⁹ Then he gave a loaf of bread, a cake of dates and a cake of raisins to each person in the whole crowd of Israelites, both men and women. And all the people went to their homes. ²⁰ When David returned home to bless his household, Michal daughter of Saul came out to meet him and said, "How the king of Israel has distinguished himself today, going around half-naked in full view of the slave girls of his servants as any vulgar fellow would!" ²¹ David said to Michal, "It was before the LORD, who chose me rather than your father or anyone from his house when he appointed me ruler over the LORD's people Israel—I will celebrate before the LORD. ²² I will become even more undignified than this, and I will be humiliated in my own eyes. But by these slave girls you spoke of, I will be held in honor." ²³ And Michal daughter of Saul had no children to the day of her death.

1 Chronicles 15:25-29

[25] So David and the elders of Israel and the commanders of units of a thousand went to bring up the ark of the covenant of the LORD from the house of Obed-Edom, with rejoicing. [26] Because God had helped the Levites who were carrying the ark of the covenant of the LORD, seven bulls and seven rams were sacrificed. [27] Now David was clothed in a robe of fine linen, as were all the Levites who were carrying the ark, and as were the musicians, and Kenaniah, who was in charge of the singing of the choirs. David also wore a linen ephod. [28] So all Israel brought up the ark of the covenant of the LORD with shouts, with the sounding of rams' horns and trumpets, and of cymbals, and the playing of lyres and harps. [29] As the ark of the covenant of the LORD was entering the City of David, Michal daughter of Saul watched from a window. And when she saw King David dancing and celebrating, she despised him in her heart.

Queen Michal was a woman who loved from a deep place. She embraced her emotions and was able to manage them well. She took the time to get to know the man that she loved and dealt with him accordingly. Women have an amazing ability to "read" the emotional climate in their relationship. Queen Michal's loving nature made her the perfect woman for a man who was destined to be King. Queen Michal's loyalty to David surpassed her loyalty to her father. Unfortunately, she allowed the remnant of her father's jealous spirit to cause her to question David's love for her and it broke her. Loving a man more than you love yourself will break you. Loving a man more than you love God will break you. Queen Michal loved from a deep place like only a woman can.

Her Leadership: Emotional Intelligent Leadership

Leaders who are in touch with their emotions are becoming emotionally intelligent and have the ability to empower themselves as leaders. Queen Michal was a woman who demonstrated emotional intelligence. Her ability to manage her emotions in the midst of loving a man who her father hated speaks volumes for her. While the Bible never talks about who and how she led, we can glean from the text that her role as Queen put her in position to influence many. According to Mayer, Caruso, & Salovey (1999) emotional intelligence is defined as an ability to validly reason with emotions and to use emotions to enhance thought. It includes the abilities to accurately perceive emotions, to access and generate emotions so as to assist thought, to understand emotions and emotional knowledge, and to reflectively regulate emotions so as to promote emotional and intellectual growth. Queen Michal was able to reason with her emotions as she used her wit to help save David from her father.

The foundation of emotional intelligence is understanding one's own cognitive, behavioral and emotional being. The cognitive, behavioral and emotional abilities relating to emotional intelligence are how we as people think, react and feel in relation to the five dimensions of emotional intelligence: self -awareness, self-management, self-motivation, empathy and the social skills used when dealing with one's self and others. The enhancement of one's cognitive, behavioral and emotional abilities helps to have success when dealing with others in many different situations. It proves profitable to have enhanced cognitive, behavioral and emotional skills because they are important when dealing with the emotional intelligence in situations and social interacting personally and professionally. People who can think, pause, and then react to situations in a positive way have better outcomes. Queen Michal's love for David did not interfere with her ability to manage her self-awareness, self-management, self-motivation, empathy, and social skills.

Our text says, "The heart of her husband safely trusts her; So he will have no lack of gain. She does him good and not evil all the days of her life. Her husband is known in the gates when he sits among the elders of the land." Loving a man from an authentic place will ultimately lead to him trusting your love for him. David knew that Queen Michal loved him and when she was taken from him and given to another man, he wouldn't rest until he got her back. Men who love the women in their lives honor the love that she has for him and treasure her for loving him well. A woman who loves a man and loves herself will have balance in her love. What is balanced love? Balanced love is emotionally intelligent in that you manage your emotions while managing the emotions of the one you love. You have self-awareness in that you will give to the man you love without depleting yourself. Your love for him will not cause you to not love yourself. You do not value your love for him more than you value his love for you. You have self-management in that you love from an authentic place. You spend time with God to bring healing in your life so that you do not love him from a broken place. You have self-motivation in that you understand what love is supposed to look like, feel like, and act like. You do not make him responsible for your joy because you understand that only God can give you that. You have empathy in that you realize that we all have a desire to love yet we get bruised when we have non-loving experiences. Empathy allows you to put yourself in the shoes of the one you love and extend grace when you want to extend anger. Finally, you have social skills in that you know that there will be times when you will give more than he will and other times when he will give more than you do. Your ability to give and receive in your relationship is reflective of your desire to love and be loved unconditionally. Queen Michal demonstrated all five dimensions throughout the course of her relationship with King David.

Your Lesson: Be a Loving Woman

Queen Michal loved David and although the Bible never says that he loved her, we see from his actions that he did. She gave up everything for him, including herself. So often women give up everything for men who do not do the same in return. The issue becomes she makes him a priority when he makes her an option. Ladies, making a man a priority when he makes you an option puts you at a major disadvantage. While I agree that love covers a multitude, I do not agree that love is enough to keep a relationship. Love must be in conjunction with trust, communication, friendship, loyalty, integrity, and faith. Love is a verb and a noun. Queen Michal walked in principle # 2, she *Named Her Truth* when she decided to betray her father, King Saul, to protect the man she loved, David. She *Named Her Truth* when she chose to love David with everything that was in her. She also *Named Her Truth* when she chose to tell David how his actions made her feel. Loving a man with all that you have is not bad in and of itself. Loving a man with everything you have when he does not love you the same way is a problem. *Naming Your Truth* means being honest with yourself about your current reality. Women love from a very deep place and when that love is not reciprocated, we have a way of making excuses for that truth. Be resolved not to attempt to live comfortably in a lie. My sister, your love has value. His love for you is not worth more than your

132

love for him. Being a loving woman means knowing who deserves your love, knowing when to give your love, and knowing that you are precious and he needs to earn the right to receive your love unconditionally.

Spiritual Position of Attention

Endurance of a Leader

LOVE IS WHO YOU ARE AND WHAT YOU DO

¹³ You also do this: You cover the altar of the LORD with tears as you weep and groan, because he no longer pays any attention to the offering nor accepts it favorably from you. ¹⁴ Yet you ask, "Why?" The LORD is testifying against you on behalf of the wife you married when you were young, to whom you have become unfaithful even though she is your companion and wife by law. ¹⁵ No one who has even a small portion of the Spirit in him does this. What did our ancestor do when seeking a child from God? Be attentive, then, to your own spirit, for one should not be disloyal to the wife he took in his youth. Malachi 2:13-15 (NET)

Peace from God:_____

_____

_____

_____

_____

My rest in
God:_____

_____

_____

_____

_____

_____

My "yes" to God:_____

_____

_____

_____

_____

Chapter Four

Principle #3
Lady On Your Own Terms

13 She seeks wool and flax, And willingly works with her hands. 14 She is like the merchant ships, She brings her food from afar. 15 She also rises while it is yet night, And provides food for her household, And a portion for her maidservants. 16 She considers a field and buys it; From her profits she plants a vineyard. 18 She perceives that her merchandise is good, And her lamp does not go out by night. 19 She stretches out her hands to the distaff, And her hand holds the spindle. 21 She is not afraid of snow for her household, For all her household is clothed with scarlet. 22 She makes tapestry for herself; Her clothing is fine linen and purple. 24 She makes linen garments and sells them, And supplies sashes for the merchants.

The choice to be who you want to be is something that some women have never been afforded. Many women have been ushered into a life that they have not chosen for themselves. Little girls are groomed to be givers, servers, life givers, helpers, followers, and the like. Amazingly, we have a continuum of teachings from "all you need is a good man" to "you never need a man". Even with all of that, we are acculturated to believe that a good man will "save" us. What do I mean by "save" you? Earlier I talked about what Collette

Dowling (1981) calls the "Cinderella Complex. She explains it this way:

> The "wish to be saved" is quite probably the most important issue facing women today. We were brought up to depend on a man and to feel naked and frightened without one. We were taught to believe that as women we cannot stand alone, that we are too fragile, too delicate, needful of protection. So that now, in these enlightened days, when our intellects tell us to stand on our own two feet, unresolved emotional issues drag us down. At the same time that we yearn to be fetterless and free, we also yearn to be taken care of.

Women who have degrees and six figures are waiting for Prince Charming. Anointed women who can pastor, preach, administrate, shepherd, and lead wait for their SMOG (Sexy Man of God) to "save" them. We have been taught that we stand on our own until "he" comes to "save" us. Even when we have multiple talents and gifts like the Proverbs 31 woman, we wrestle with standing in the fullness of who we are in the face of loving a man or being loved by a man. Verses 13-16; 18-19; 21-22; and 24 describes an innovative woman. She had an array of abilities and was able to do all of them well. This woman understood that who she was and what she brought to the table had value. Principle #3 is Lady on Your Own Terms. You decide who you are and what you want to do. This principle will be illuminated through Queen Vashti. She is an innovative woman who demonstrated transformational leadership.

The Lady: Queen Vashti

Queen Vashti was a woman who had a mind of her own. She knew what she wanted and did not waver regardless of the consequences. She chose her path and was not afraid to stand her ground. She appears in Esther 1 and 2.

Esther 1:9-22

[9] Queen Vashti also gave a banquet for the women in the palace which belonged to King Ahasuerus. [10] On the seventh day, when the heart of the king was merry with wine, he commanded Mehuman, Biztha, Harbona, Bigtha, Abagtha, Zethar and Carkas, the seven eunuchs who served in the presence of King Ahasuerus, [11] to bring Queen Vashti before the king with her royal crown in order to display her beauty to the people and the princes, for she was

beautiful. [12]But Queen Vashti refused to come at the king's command delivered by the eunuchs. Then the king became very angry and his wrath burned within him. [13]Then the king said to the wise men who understood the times--for it was the custom of the king so to speak before all who knew law and justice [14]and were close to him: Carshena, Shethar, Admatha, Tarshish, Meres, Marsena and Memucan, the seven princes of Persia and Media who had access to the king's presence and sat in the first place in the kingdom-- "According to law, what is to be done with Queen Vashti, because she did not obey the command of King Ahasuerus delivered by the eunuchs?" [16]In the presence of the king and the princes, Memucan said, "Queen Vashti has wronged not only the king but also all the princes and all the peoples who are in all the provinces of King Ahasuerus. "For the queen's conduct will become known to all the women causing them to look with contempt on their husbands by saying, 'King Ahasuerus commanded Queen Vashti to be brought in to his presence, but she did not come.' "This day the ladies of Persia and Media who have heard of the queen's conduct will speak in the same way to all the king's princes, and there will be plenty of contempt and anger. "If it pleases the king, let a royal edict be issued by him and let it be written in the laws of Persia and Media so that it cannot be repealed, that Vashti may no longer come into the presence of King Ahasuerus, and let the king give her royal position to another who is more worthy than she. "When the king's edict which he will make is heard throughout all his kingdom, great as it is, then all women will give honor to their husbands, great and small." This word pleased the king and the princes, and the king did as Memucan proposed. ²²So he sent letters to all the king's provinces, to each province according to its script and to every people according to their language, that every man should be the master in his own house and the one who speaks in the language of his own people.

Esther 2:1
After these things when the anger of King Ahasuerus had subsided, he remembered Vashti and what she had done and what had been decreed against her.

Esther 2:17
And the king loved Esther more than all the other women, and she met with his loving approval more than all the other young women.

So he placed the royal high turban on her head and appointed her queen in place of Vashti.

Queen Vashti's story is like so many women in the Bible, told for her. This woman was so amazing that her actions put fear in men. One act changed the course of history. Queen Vashti's decision to honor herself and not parade her beauty at the King's bequest was so powerful that the men in power believed it would touch every woman in the province. Even though the Bible does not share details about Queen Vashti's leadership, we do know that her influence on the women in her realm demonstrated her leadership. Her skills and abilities were so great that the men found it necessary to make marginalizing women the law of the land. Clearly she was innovative as the above verses describe. She was a transformational leader that touched the lives of women and men.

Her Leadership: Transformational

Transformational leadership is the leader's intentional practice of empowering those that follow them with information, opportunities for application, and inspiration to keep trying.

According to Bass and 0Riggio (2006) transformational leaders motivate others to do more than they originally intended and often even more than they thought possible. The leadership inspires followers with challenge and persuasion, providing both meaning and understanding. The leadership is intellectually stimulating, expanding the followers' use of their abilities. Transformational leaders behave in ways that allow them to serve as role models and inspire their followers. Inspiration goes a long way. Leaders who have the ability to inspire followers get a lot done. A major part of inspiration is helping people realize their dreams. Kouzes and Posner (2012) say:

> Leaders are dreamers. Leaders are idealists. Leaders are possibility thinkers. All enterprises, big or small, begin with the belief that what's merely an image today, can one day be made real. It's this belief that sustains leaders through the difficult times. Turning possibility thinking into an inspiring vision-and one that is shared-is another of your challenges as a leader.

Only transformational leaders are comfortable enough to allow other people to dream because they understand that helping others reach their dreams helps them reach their own dreams. Queen Vashti made a bold move when she disobeyed her husband's request. She understood her value and all of her gifts and talents. She chose not to minimize herself and in doing that she became a transformer of her time.

Your Lesson: Be an Innovative Woman

Innovative women know who they are and what gifts they bring to the table. They know that they may be perceived as "too much" or "extra". The value is not tied to whether or not people like them. These women make a conscious decision to develop each gift to the best of their ability. They make no excuses for being multi-talented and choose not to minimize their abilities. According to McKenzie (2002)

> Learned ignorance is a crutch that some people use. They deliberately appear ignorant or helpless when they are not. They think the same way they've always thought or think the

same way the people around them think because it's easier than thinking for themselves. Learned helplessness, a kissing cousin of learned ignorance, does not mean that a person is incapable; it means she does not want to do it on her own. Many women spend their lives in learned ignorance, the deliberate decision not to know, not to respond, not to avail themselves of knowledge and information. Learned ignorance leads to intentionally ignoring invitations and opportunities, the too convenient excuse for wasted intelligence, skill, and talent.

Learned ignorance and learned helplessness are not a part of an innovative women's vocabulary or makeup. She is centered within herself and her abilities. There is a special humility that comes with having an abundance of ability. Queen Vashti knew her worth and we must move to a place where we know ours. The King's edict that women should be subject to their husbands that went throughout his providence is still being felt today. Just as the decree went all over the province then, dishonoring and devaluing of women can be felt all over the world today. There are men who know and embrace the worth of a good woman. Min. Louis Farrakan shares what Islam teaches:

> Without you we wouldn't be, without you by our side we could never achieve. The Honorable Elijah Muhammad said, "No nation can rise any higher than its woman. So if you put your woman down, you go down with her. If you lift your woman up, you go up with her. So our disrespect of our women is a part of the self-hatred of us as men. Our women demand from us what we can't give because we're broken men. So in the Nation of Islam and the teachings of the Honorable Elijah Muhammad he teaches the woman how to help the man be the man that he should be that she can fall in love with him, honor him, and respect him because he is becoming a man. How do you know he's becoming a man, because he is becoming more like God. I could not be who I am if God didn't give me a woman to help me be what I am. My dear sisters, you have to learn how to respect yourself. You are not just a woman, you are a sacred vessel. I'm not trying to put women on a pedestal that they don't deserve to be on. No man is a man without a woman. It's the woman

who helps the man be a man. A man who doesn't have a woman doesn't know if he is one. What do I mean by that? A woman will test you to see if you are what you say you are. Any woman that you fall in love with, she loves you too but she is going to try you. That's her nature, she's gotta know if she can depend on you. She gotta know that you will stand up for her.

An innovative woman needs a man in her life who loves her celebrates who she is becoming. The Spiritual Alpha Female gives God credit for who she is and all that she is able to do. There is no room for self-aggrandizement, promoting oneself as powerful. The innovative woman connects her power to God.

Spiritual Position of Attention

Execution of a Leader

YOU CANNOT LEAD FROM BEHIND

For I know what I have planned for you says the Lord. I have plans to prosper you, not to harm you. I have plans to give you a future filled with hope. When you call out to me and come to me in prayer, I will hear your prayers. When you seek me in prayer and worship, you will find me available to you. If you seek me with all your heart and soul, I will make myself available to you says the Lord. Jeremiah 29: 11-14a (NET)

Peace from God:_____

_____

_____

_____

_____

My rest in God:_____

_____

_____

_____

_____

_____

My "yes" to God:_____

_____

_____

_____

_____

Chapter Five

Principle #4 Evident Integrity

17 She girds herself with strength, and strengthens her arms. 25 Strength and honor are her clothing; She shall rejoice in time to come. 26 She opens her mouth with wisdom, and on her tongue is the law of kindness.

Integrity happens. It is the intentional internal mandate to live an honorable life whether people are watching or not. It is that desire to live above reproach because it is the least you can do to honor an amazing God. A woman of integrity is wise beyond her years and has no need to wrestle with who she is to God and to others. Principle #4 is Integrity. A woman of integrity is in constant communion with God to keep her supply of wisdom ongoing and kind at its core. The Bible gives us a glimpse of women who walk in integrity. Unfortunately, the greatest examples never speak for themselves. This principle will be illuminated through the life of Queen Bathsheba. She is a wise woman who demonstrated primal leadership.

The Lady: Queen Bathsheba

Queen Bathsheba was a woman who was married to a soldier yet the King saw her, wanted her, and had sex with her. She became pregnant and the King had her husband killed. God's chastisement to David was that their would die. In her sadness King David comforted her and they were blessed with King Solomon. Queen Bathsheba had no say in the course of any of these events. She had a tough beginning as a Queen yet she remained true to herself and true to her God. Her story is told in 2 Samuel 11, 2 Samuel 12, 1 Kings 1, 1 Kings 2, 1 Chronicles 3, Psalm 51, and Matthew 1.

2 Samuel 11:3

Now when evening came David arose from his bed and walked around on the roof of the king's house, and from the roof he saw a woman bathing; and the woman was very beautiful in appearance. [3] So David sent and inquired about the woman. And one said, "Is this not Bathsheba, the daughter of Eliam, the wife of Uriah the Hittite?" [4] David sent messengers and took her, and when she came to him, he lay with her; and when she had purified herself from her uncleanness, she returned to her house. **5** The woman conceived; and she sent and told David, and said, "I am pregnant." **6** Then David sent to Joab, *saying*, "Send me Uriah the Hittite." So Joab sent Uriah to David. **7** When Uriah came to him, David asked concerning the welfare of Joab and the people and the state of the war. **8** Then David said to Uriah, "Go down to your house, and wash your feet." And Uriah went out of the king's house, and a present from the king was sent out after him. **9** But Uriah slept at the door of the king's house with all the servants of his lord, and did not go down to his house. **10** Now when they told David, saying, "Uriah did not go down to his house," David said to Uriah, "Have you not come from a journey? Why did you not go down to your house?" **11** Uriah said to David, "The ark and Israel and Judah are staying in temporary shelters, and my lord Joab and the servants of my lord are camping in the open field. Shall I then go to my house to eat and to drink and to lie with my wife? By your life and the life of your soul, I will not do this thing." **12** Then David said to Uriah, "Stay here today also, and tomorrow I will let you go." So Uriah remained in Jerusalem that day and the next. **13** Now David called him, and he ate and drank

---

before him, and he made him drunk; and in the evening he went out to lie on his bed with his lord's servants, but he did not go down to his house. ¹⁴ Now in the morning David wrote a letter to Joab and sent it by the hand of Uriah. ¹⁵ He had written in the letter, saying, "Place Uriah in the front line of the fiercest battle and withdraw from him, so that he may be struck down and die." ¹⁶ So it was as Joab kept watch on the city, that he put Uriah at the place where he knew there were valiant men. ¹⁷ The men of the city went out and fought against Joab, and some of the people among David's servants fell; and Uriah the Hittite also died.¹⁸ Then Joab sent and reported to David all the events of the war. ¹⁹ He charged the messenger, saying, "When you have finished telling all the events of the war to the king, ²⁰ and if it happens that the king's wrath rises and he says to you, 'Why did you go so near to the city to fight? Did you not know that they would shoot from the wall? ²¹ Who struck down Abimelech the son of Jerubbesheth? Did not a woman throw an upper millstone on him from the wall so that he died at Thebez? Why did you go so near the wall?'—then you shall say, 'Your servant Uriah the Hittite is dead also.'" ²² So the messenger departed and came and reported to David all that

Joab had sent him *to* tell. ²³ The messenger said to David, "The men prevailed against us and came out against us in the field, but we pressed them as far as the entrance of the gate. ²⁴ Moreover, the archers shot at your servants from the wall; so some of the king's servants are dead, and your servant Uriah the Hittite is also dead."²⁵ Then David said to the messenger, "Thus you shall say to Joab, 'Do not let this thing displease you, for the sword devours one as well as another; make your battle against the city stronger and overthrow it'; and so encourage him." ²⁶ Now when the wife of Uriah heard that Uriah her husband was dead, she mourned for her husband. ²⁷ When the time of mourning was over, David sent and brought her to his house and she became his wife; then she bore him a son. But the thing that David had done was evil in the sight of the LORD.

2 Samuel 12

Then the LORD struck the child that Uriah's widow bore to David, so that he was very sick. ¹⁶ David therefore inquired of God for the child; and David fasted and went and lay all night on the ground. ¹⁷ The elders of his household stood beside him in order to raise him up from the ground, but he was unwilling and would not eat food with them. [18] Then it happened on the seventh day that the child died. And the servants of David were afraid to tell him that the child was dead, for they said, "Behold, while the child was still alive, we spoke to him and he did not listen to our voice. How then can we tell him that the child is dead, since he might do himself harm!" [19] But when David saw that his servants were whispering together, David perceived that the child was dead; so David said to his servants, "Is the child dead?" And they said, "He is dead." [20] So David arose from the ground, washed, anointed himself, and changed his clothes; and he came into the house of the LORD and worshiped. Then he came to his own house, and when he requested, they set food before him and he ate. [21] Then his servants said to him, "What is this thing that you have done? While the child was alive, you fasted and wept; but when the child died, you arose and ate food." [22] He said, "While the child was still alive, I fasted and wept; for I said, 'Who knows, the LORD may be gracious to me, that the child may live.' [23] But now he has died; why should I fast? Can I bring him back again? I will go to him, but he will not return to me." Then David comforted his wife Bathsheba, and he went to her and made love to her. She gave

birth to a son, and they named him Solomon. The Lord loved him;

1 Kings 1:11-31

Then Nathan spoke to Bathsheba the mother of Solomon, saying,

"Have you not heard that Adonijah the son of Haggith has become

king, and David our lord does not know it? ¹² So now come, please

let me give you counsel and save your life and the life of your son

Solomon. ¹³ Go at once to King David and say to him, 'Have you

not, my lord, O king, sworn to your maidservant, saying, "Surely

Solomon your son shall be king after me, and he shall sit on my

throne"? Why then has Adonijah become king?' ¹⁴ "Behold, while

you are still there speaking with the king, I will come in after you

and confirm your words." ¹⁵ So Bathsheba went in to the king in

the bedroom. Now the king was very old, and Abishag the

Shunammite was ministering to the king.¹⁶ Then Bathsheba bowed

and prostrated herself before the king. And the king said, "What do

you wish?" ¹⁷ She said to him, "My lord, you swore to your

maidservant by the LORD your God, saying, 'Surely your son

Solomon shall be king after me and he shall sit on my

throne.'[18] Now, behold, Adonijah is king; and now, my lord the king, you do not know *it*. [19] He has sacrificed oxen and fatlings and sheep in abundance, and has invited all the sons of the king and Abiathar the priest and Joab the commander of the army, but he has not invited Solomon your servant. [20] As for you now, my lord the king, the eyes of all Israel are on you, to tell them who shall sit on the throne of my lord the king after him. [21] Otherwise it will come about, as soon as my lord the king sleeps with his fathers, that I and my son Solomon will be considered offenders."

[22] Behold, while she was still speaking with the king, Nathan the prophet came in. [23] They told the king, saying, "Here is Nathan the prophet." And when he came in before the king, he prostrated himself before the king with his face to the ground. [24] Then Nathan said, "My lord the king, have you said, 'Adonijah shall be king after me, and he shall sit on my throne'? [25] For he has gone down today and has sacrificed oxen and fatlings and sheep in abundance, and has invited all the king's sons and the commanders of the army and Abiathar the priest, and behold, they are eating and drinking before him; and they say, 'Long live King Adonijah!' [26] But me, even me your servant, and Zadok the priest and Benaiah the

son of Jehoiada and your servant Solomon, he has not

invited. ²⁷ Has this thing been done by my lord the king, and you

have not shown to your servants who should sit on the throne of

my lord the king after him?" ²⁸ Then King David said, "Call

Bathsheba to me." And she came into the king's presence and

stood before the king. ²⁹ The king vowed and said, "As

the LORD lives, who has redeemed my life from all

distress, ³⁰ surely as I vowed to you by the LORD the God of Israel,

saying, 'Your son Solomon shall be king after me, and he shall sit

on my throne in my place'; I will indeed do so this day." ³¹ Then

Bathsheba bowed with her face to the ground, and prostrated

herself before the king and said, "May my lord King David live

forever."

1 Kings 2:13

Now Adonijah the son of Haggith came to Bathsheba the mother

of Solomon. And she said, "Do you come peacefully?" And he

said, "Peacefully." ¹⁴ Then he said, "I have something to say to

you." And she said, "Speak." ¹⁵ So he said, "You know that the

kingdom was mine and that all Israel expected me to be

king; however, the kingdom has turned about and become my brother's, for it was his from the LORD. [16] Now I am making one request of you; do not refuse me." And she said to him, "Speak." [17] Then he said, "Please speak to Solomon the king, for he will not refuse you, that he may give me Abishag the Shunammite as a wife." [18] Bathsheba said, "Very well; I will speak to the king for you." [19] So Bathsheba went to King Solomon to speak to him for Adonijah. And the king arose to meet her, bowed before her, and sat on his throne; then he had a throne set for the king's mother, and she sat on his right. [20] Then she said, "I am making one small request of you; do not refuse me." And the king said to her, "Ask, my mother, for I will not refuse you." [21] So she said, "Let Abishag the Shunammite be given to Adonijah your brother as a wife." [22] King Solomon answered and said to his mother, "And why are you asking Abishag the Shunammite for Adonijah? Ask for him also the kingdom—for he is my older brother—even for him, for Abiathar the priest, and for Joab the son of Zeruiah!" [23] Then King Solomon swore by the LORD, saying, "May God do so to me and more also, if Adonijah has not spoken this word against his own life. [24] Now therefore, as the LORD lives, who has established me and set me on the throne of David my father and who has made me a house as He promised, surely Adonijah shall be put to death today." [25] So King Solomon sent Benaiah the son of Jehoiada; and he fell upon him so that he died.

1 Chronicles 3:5

These were born to him in Jerusalem: Shimea, Shobab, Nathan and Solomon, four, by Bath-shua the daughter of Ammiel;

Her Leadership: Primal Leadership

Queen Bathsheba was a primal leader, meaning intrinsic and inherent in her abilities. A primal leader is one who handles themselves and their relationships with emotional intelligence. They drive the emotions of the people they lead in the right direction. According to Goleman, Boyatzis, and McKee (2013) no matter what leaders set out to do-whether it's creating strategy or mobilizing teams to action-their success depends on how they do it. Even if they get everything else just right, if leaders fail in this primal task of driving emotions in the right direction, nothing they do will work as well as it could or should. Queen Bathsheba was able to remain kind and extend kindness even though she had no say in King David having sex with her, getting her pregnant, killing her husband, marrying her, and having more children with her. She did this through her primal ability to drive her emotions in a positive direction. Even though I love the idea of using emotions, I am very clear that what can be used for good can also be used for bad. Leaders in general have to choose how they lead and how they will handle their own emotions as well as the emotions of others. Resonance, *driving emotion positively*, and dissonance, *driving emotion negatively* set the tone for how leaders use emotional intelligence. Resonant leaders use wisdom undergirded with kindness. Proverbs 31:25 speaks to wearing strength as a garment. It takes immeasurable strength to manage your own emotions in a positive manner in the face of the many challenges in life.

One of the things that I found the most fascinating about primal leadership is the focus on the brain. It amazes me how God created the complexities of the brain. We have an innate ability to mirror emotions and use it to bring ease to any given situation. According to Rodin (2002) the reason a leader's manner-not just what he does, but *how* he does it-matters so much lies in the design of the human brain: what scientists have begun to call the *open-loop* nature of the limbic system, our emotional centers. A closed loop system such as the circulatory system is self-regulating; what's happening in the circulatory system of others around us does not impact our own system. An open-loop system depends largely on the external sources to manage itself. Queen Bathsheba was able to mirror emotion on a number of occasions that worked in her favor. This open and closed loop speaks volumes to the success and failure of the primal leader. The foundational truth of the leader is to utilize the brains ability to *mirror* the emotion of the followers in an effort to lead in a positive way. Although this has a level of fascination it also has a level of fear. I say this because a closed loop has minimal variables. There is no opportunity for outside influences that could or would alter the outcome of the system. The open-loop on the other hand has many variables and possibilities that can ultimately change the course of the system at any given time. The very thing that is designed to help people manage themselves leaves them open to be negatively influenced and mismanaged.

When it comes primal leadership, the focus on the emotion is a tricky one. Being emotion focused can bring healing and it can bring harm. Emotions can do damage and I have seen it happen on many occasions. I believe that that is why emotions are suppressed. The *emotional hijacking* is a big issue. The issue happens in families, in churches, in organizations, and in communities. How often do we hear the term *one bad apple spoils the whole bunch?* All it takes is one person to sow a seed of dissonance and before you know it chaos and pandemonium happens. The images that we use, the language that we manipulate, and the marginalizing leadership styles that we use hold people hostage on many levels. *Emotional hijacking* makes it next to impossible for people to be emotionally intelligent. It gets increasingly difficult to differentiate between authentic emotion and hijacked emotion. Spiritual Alpha Females understand the power they hold as emotionally intelligent women. They are intentional about using words that heal instead of hurt. Proverbs 31:26 speaks of using kind words of wisdom. When I think about leadership, what comes to mind is language and how we use language to heal or to hurt. Leaders have the distinct role of finding the right language at the right time for the right people. I have encountered leaders who use language to hold their followers hostage to their agenda. It never ceases to amaze me how influential we are to each other. Resonate leaders use loving wise language to hold the heart of the people in their hands while dissonant leaders use disheartening language to grip the heart of the people in their hands. The greatest difference between the two is how the heart of the followers is handled. Resonant leaders understand and value the influence that they have in the lives of the people. They honor the covenant that they have with God to lead and love those that follow them. Dissonant leaders place higher value on the manipulation that they enforce to get what they want. Their covenant with God's has little or no impact in their lives. The Spiritual Alpha Female chooses to be a resonant leader just as Queen Bathsheba did.

Your Lesson: Be a Wise Woman

Being a woman of integrity calls upon the primal love spirit that we were created in. We mirror the image and likeness of love. It is a wise choice to call upon the deepest part of who you are, love. Wisdom comes with experience and time. My beloved sister, your life has taught you invaluable lessons about what to do and what not to do. Your past should not dictate your use of loving wisdom language and behavior. Queen Bathsheba was raped by the King. He did not ask if she wanted to have sex, she had no choice. I am sure that she had some rough nights because of what she had been through, yet she prevailed as a wise loving woman who raised the wisest King to ever live. She was revered so that when she went to talk with her son he rose to greet her, bowed before her, and set a throne for her on his right side. Queen Bathsheba demonstrated integrating integrity in her life regardless of the pain of her past. It is your choice now to do the same.

Spiritual Position of Attention

Enrichment of a Leader

YOUR STORY IS YOUR STORY

Every wise woman builds her household, but a foolish woman tears
it down with her own hands.
Proverbs 14:1 (NET)

Peace from God:_____

_____

_____

_____

_____

My rest in God:_____

_____

_____

_____

_____

My "yes" to God:_____

_____

_____

_____

_____

Chapter Six

Principle #5 Accentuate Kindness

20 She extends her hand to the poor, Yes, she reaches out her hands to the needy.

Kindness is something that comes from the core of who you are. The core of who we are is love. God is love. We are created in the image and likeness of God. Society teaches that extending kindness is something that must be earned. Faith teaches us that extending kindness is the least we can do in response to a loving God who extends kindness to us. Principle #5 is Accentuate Kindness. This principle will be illuminated through Queen Abigail. She is a kind woman who demonstrated path-goal leadership.

The Lady: Queen Abigail

Queen Abigail was a woman who had no choice in marrying a fool prior to meeting and marrying King David. She was a woman who did not allow non-loving experiences to make her heart bitter. Bitterness is the enemy of kindness in that it eats away at your spirit of love. Queen Abigail's story can be found in: 1 Samuel 25, 1 Samuel 27, 1 Samuel 30, 2 Samuel 3, and 1 Chronicles 3.

1 Sam 25

Now Samuel died, and all Israel assembled and mourned for him; and they buried him at his home in Ramah. Then David moved down into the Desert of Paran. [2] A certain man in Maon, who had property there at Carmel, was very wealthy. He had a thousand goats and three thousand sheep, which he was shearing in Carmel. [3] His name was Nabal and his wife's name was Abigail. She was an intelligent and beautiful woman, but her husband was surly and mean in his dealings—he was a Calebite. [4] While David was in the wilderness, he heard that Nabal was shearing sheep. [5] So he sent ten young men and said to them, "Go up to Nabal at Carmel and greet him in my name. [6] Say to him: 'Long life to you! Good health to you and your household! And good health to all that is yours! [7] ""Now I hear that it is sheep-shearing time. When your shepherds were with us, we did not mistreat them, and the whole time they were at Carmel nothing of theirs was missing. [8] Ask your own servants and they will tell you. Therefore be favorable toward my men, since we come at a festive time. Please give your servants and your son David whatever you can find for them.'" ⁹ When David's men arrived, they gave Nabal this message in David's name. Then they waited. ¹⁰ Nabal answered David's servants, "Who is this David? Who is this son of Jesse? Many servants are breaking away from their masters these days. ¹¹ Why should I take my bread and water, and the meat I have slaughtered for my shearers, and give it to men coming from who knows where?" ¹² David's men turned around and went back. When they arrived, they reported every word. ¹³ David said to his men, "Each of you strap on your sword!" So they did, and David strapped his on as well. About four hundred men went up with David, while two hundred stayed with the supplies. ¹⁴ One of the servants told Abigail, Nabal's wife, "David sent messengers from the wilderness to give our master his greetings, but he hurled insults at them. ¹⁵ Yet these men were very good to us. They did not mistreat us, and the whole time we were out in the fields near them nothing was missing. ¹⁶ Night and day they were a wall around us the whole time we were herding our sheep near them. ¹⁷ Now think it over and see what you can do, because disaster is hanging over our master and his whole household. He is such a wicked man that no one can talk to him."

¹⁸ Abigail acted quickly. She took two hundred loaves of bread, two skins of wine, five dressed sheep, five seahs of roasted grain, a hundred cakes of raisins and two hundred cakes of pressed figs, and loaded them on donkeys. ¹⁹ Then she told her servants, "Go on ahead; I'll follow you." But she did not tell her husband Nabal. ²⁰ As she came riding her donkey into a mountain ravine, there were David and his men descending toward her, and she met them. ²¹ David had just said, "It's been useless—all my watching over this fellow's property in the wilderness so that nothing of his was missing. He has paid me back evil for good. ²² May God deal with David, be it ever so severely, if by morning I leave alive one male of all who belong to him!" ²³ When Abigail saw David, she quickly got off her donkey and bowed down before David with her face to the ground. ²⁴ She fell at his feet and said: "Pardon your servant, my lord, and let me speak to you; hear what your servant has to say. ²⁵ Please pay no attention, my lord, to that wicked man Nabal. He is just like his name—his name means Fool, and folly goes with him. And as for me, your servant, I did not see the men my lord sent. ²⁶ And now, my lord, as surely as the LORD your God lives and as you live, since the LORD has kept you from bloodshed and from

avenging yourself with your own hands, may your enemies and all who are intent on harming my lord be like Nabal. ²⁷ And let this gift, which your servant has brought to my lord, be given to the men who follow you. ²⁸ "Please forgive your servant's presumption. The LORD your God will certainly make a lasting dynasty for my lord, because you fight the LORD's battles, and no wrongdoing will be found in you as long as you live. ²⁹ Even though someone is pursuing you to take your life, the life of my lord will be bound securely in the bundle of the living by the LORD your God, but the lives of your enemies he will hurl away as from the pocket of a sling. ³⁰ When the LORD has fulfilled for my lord every good thing he promised concerning him and has appointed him ruler over Israel, ³¹ my lord will not have on his conscience the staggering burden of needless bloodshed or of having avenged himself. And when the LORD your God has brought my lord success, remember your servant."

³² David said to Abigail, "Praise be to the LORD, the God of Israel, who has sent you today to meet me. ³³ May you be blessed for your good judgment and for keeping me from bloodshed this day and from avenging myself with my own hands. ³⁴ Otherwise, as surely as the LORD, the God of Israel, lives, who has kept me from

harming you, if you had not come quickly to meet me, not one male belonging to Nabal would have been left alive by daybreak."

³⁵ Then David accepted from her hand what she had brought him and said, "Go home in peace. I have heard your words and granted your request." ³⁶ When Abigail went to Nabal, he was in the house holding a banquet like that of a king. He was in high spirits and very drunk. So she told him nothing at all until daybreak. ³⁷ Then in the morning, when Nabal was sober, his wife told him all these things, and his heart failed him and he became like a stone.

³⁸ About ten days later, the LORD struck Nabal and he died.

³⁹ When David heard that Nabal was dead, he said, "Praise be to the LORD, who has upheld my cause against Nabal for treating me with contempt. He has kept his servant from doing wrong and has brought Nabal's wrongdoing down on his own head." Then David sent word to Abigail, asking her to become his wife. ⁴⁰ His servants went to Carmel and said to Abigail, "David has sent us to you to take you to become his wife." ⁴¹ She bowed down with her face to the ground and said, "I am your servant and am ready to serve you and wash the feet of my lord's servants." ⁴² Abigail quickly got on a donkey and, attended by her five female servants, went with

David's messengers and became his wife. ⁴³ David had also married Ahinoam of Jezreel, and they both were his wives. ⁴⁴ But Saul had given his daughter Michal, David's wife, to Paltiel son of Laish, who was from Gallim.

1 Samuel 27:3

And David lived with Achish at Gath, he and his men, each with his household, *even* David with his two wives, Ahinoam the Jezreelitess, and Abigail the Carmelitess, Nabal's widow.

1 Samuel 30:5

Now David's two wives had been taken captive, Ahinoam the Jezreelitess and Abigail the widow of Nabal the Carmelite.

2 Samuel 2:2

So David went up there, and his two wives also, Ahinoam the Jezreelitess and Abigail the widow of Nabal the Carmelite.

2 Samuel 3:3

² Now sons were born to David in Hebron. His firstborn was Amnon, born to Ahinoam the Jezreelite. ³ and his second, Chileab, by Abigail the widow of Nabal the Carmelite; and the third, Absalom the son of Maacah, the daughter of Talmai, king of Geshur;

1 Chronicles 3:1

Now these were the sons of David who were born to him in Hebron: the firstborn *was* Amnon, by Ahinoam the Jezreelitess; the second *was* Daniel, by Abigail the Carmelitess;

Queen Abigail was a woman who understood who she belonged to. Unlike many other Queens, she spoke. Like Queen Sheba, she spoke profound words that were received by the King. She was very clear that God was her center and her words and actions lined up with that. One thing that sets Queen Abigail apart from the other Queens is that she was asked if she wanted to be the King's wife. He pursued her because he saw something in her that blessed his life. King David is a good example of a man who understood that he was finding a good thing. She saved King David from himself and found favor in his eyes. The kindness that she displayed came from the core of who she was. Spiritual Alpha Females are kind without reservation as to whether the recipient deserves it or not. Kindness is a part of the fabric of who they are.

Her Leadership: Path-Goal Leadership

The complexities associated with leadership make room for a plethora of leadership styles that become good examples of patience, openness, and empathy. Empathy involves putting yourself in the shoes of another in an effort to feel with them. Leaders must be intentional about utilizing the proper leadership style to maintain empathy for those that they lead. The path-goal theory makes sense to me when we talk about being an empathetic leader. Northouse (2013) shares the path–goal theory emphasizes the relationship between the leader's style and the characteristics of the followers and the organizational setting. For the leader, the imperative is to use a leadership style that best meets followers' motivational needs. Queen Abigail demonstrated this leadership style in her dealings with saving King David and telling her husband Nabal what he had done. The path-goal theory reminds me of Jesus' approach to leading His disciples. I recall the story of Jesus in John 21:15-17 where he said to Peter "Do you love me"? Jesus asked the question three times and Peter's response was the same all three times. Jesus changed the question by the third time. The first two times Jesus used the Greek work *agape* which talks about unconditional Godly love. Peter responded with *eros* which talks about a conditional friendship kind of love. As Jesus asked the question and saw that Peter was not following He used the language that Peter used. Now does that mean that Jesus meant less or does that mean that Jesus decided to meet Peter where he was? Essentially, Jesus was empathetic and used path-goal theory. Jesus did shift according to what Peter could handle as well as recognize that His leadership is only leadership with followship.

Leadership from an empathetic path-goal perspective lends itself to the psychodynamic approach which focuses on the dynamics of human behavior. Northouse (2013) shared:

The psychodynamic approach to leadership study and development focuses on the dynamics of human behavior, which are often the most difficult to understand. It acknowledges that people are complex, unique, and paradoxical beings with rich and myriad motivational drivers and decision-making and interaction patterns. Applying psychodynamic concepts to the ebb and flow of life in organizations contributes to our understanding of the vicissitudes of life and leadership.

It never ceases to amaze me that leadership is reciprocal. Queen Abigail led King David and he followed her. Her ability to mirror his emotions and use a psychodynamic approach made her an exceptional path-goal leader.

Leadership and followship go hand in hand. Empathy in leadership helps foster loyal and positive followship. Leaders need to be aware and sensitive to their own empathy as well as their followers' empathy. According to Hardy (1995) leaders must:

Recognize and attend to the distinction between awareness and sensitivity. Awareness is primarily a cognitive function; an individual becomes conscious of a thought or action and processes it intellectually. Sensitivity, on the other hand, is primarily an affective function; an individual responds emotionally to stimuli with delicacy and respectfulness. Although these functions appear unique and separate, each is shaded with nuances of the other. Essentially, awareness involves a conscious sensitivity, and sensitivity involves a delicate awareness.

The ability to be aware and sensitive is the amazing part of being an empathetic path-goal leader. Queen Abigail had an awareness of who God was in her life and sensitivity to the influence that God had given her as a leader.

Your Lesson: Be a Kind Woman

Kindness calls upon the self-less part of us. It ushers us to a place of unconditional love as we think about how kind God is to us. The Bible talks about God's lovingkindness on many occasions. The New American Standard Version of the Bible mentions it 182 times. The challenge for us is that we are acculturated to believe that there is no need to attach loving to kindness. Kindness is not authentic without love. Loving God and accepting God's spirit of love into your life gives you the ability to tap into the loving spirit inside of you. Tapping into God's spirit of love keeps you from choosing who gets kindness and who does not. Queen Abigail was kind to King David as well as her husband Nabal. Proverbs 31:20

talks about extending kindness. Spiritual Alpha Females understand and embrace that it is a stretch of our faith and a reach of our heart to be kind to those who deserve it and those who do not.

Spiritual Position of Attention

Elements of a Leader

YOUR PATH IS YOUR PATH

I will say, 'My dear children of Israel, keep in mind the road you took when you were carried off. Mark off in your minds the landmarks. Make a mental note of telltale signs marking the way back. Return, my dear children of Israel. Return to these cities of yours. [22] How long will you vacillate, you who were once like an unfaithful daughter? For I, the LORD, promise to bring about something new on the earth, something as unique as a woman protecting a man!'
Jeremiah 31:21-22 (NET)

Peace from God:_____
_____
_____
_____
_____

My rest in God:_____
_____
_____
_____
_____

My "yes" to God:_____
_____
_____
_____
_____

184

Chapter Seven

Principle #6 Servant's Heart

27 She watches over the ways of her household, And does not eat the bread of idleness. 28 Her children rise up and call her blessed; Her husband also, and he praises her:

Queen Esther is the only Queen who has a book named after her. While the book never says that she had children it does talk about how much her husband King Xerxes loved her. Principle # 6 is Servant's Heart. It takes a deep level of love to serve from an authentic place with no expectation of anything in return. This principle will be illuminated through Queen Esther. She is a surrendered woman who demonstrated servant leadership.

The Lady: Queen Esther

Queen Esther, the only queen to have a book of the Bible named after her, became the replacement queen for King Xerxes after Queen Vashti refused the king's command to appear before him. She was a Hebrew woman named Hadassah who lived in Persia with her Uncle Mordecai after her parents died. Hadassah was a part of and won the first beauty pageant. Her story is the core of the Jewish festival of Purim. Her story is found throughout the book of Esther. We will look at Esther 2, 4, 5, and 7.

Esther 2:5-19

[5] Now there was in the citadel of Susa a Jew of the tribe of Benjamin, named Mordecai son of Jair, the son of Shimei, the son of Kish, [6] who had been carried into exile from Jerusalem by Nebuchadnezzar king of Babylon, among those taken captive with Jehoiachin King of Judah. [7] Mordecai had a cousin named Hadassah, whom he had brought up because she had neither father nor mother. This young woman, who was also known as Esther, had a lovely figure and was beautiful. Mordecai had taken her as his own daughter when her father and mother died. [8] When the king's order and edict had been proclaimed, many young women were brought to the citadel of Susa and put under the care of Hegai. Esther also was taken to the king's palace and entrusted to Hegai, who had charge of the harem. [9] She pleased him and won his favor. Immediately he provided her with her beauty treatments

and special food. He assigned to her seven female attendants selected from the king's palace and moved her and her attendants into the best place in the harem. [10] Esther had not revealed her nationality and family background, because Mordecai had forbidden her to do so. [11] Every day he walked back and forth near the courtyard of the harem to find out how Esther was and what was happening to her. [12] Before a young woman's turn came to go in to King Xerxes, she had to complete twelve months of beauty treatments prescribed for the women, six months with oil of myrrh and six with perfumes and cosmetics. [13] And this is how she would go to the king: Anything she wanted was given her to take with her from the harem to the king's palace. [14] In the evening she would go there and in the morning return to another part of the harem to the care of Shaashgaz, the king's eunuch who was in charge of the concubines. She would not return to the king unless he was pleased with her and summoned her by name. [15] When the turn came for Esther (the young woman Mordecai had adopted, the daughter of his uncle Abihail) to go to the king, she asked for nothing other than what Hegai, the king's eunuch who was in charge of the harem, suggested. And Esther won the favor of everyone who saw her. ¹⁶ She was taken to King Xerxes in the royal residence in the tenth month, the month of Tebeth, in the seventh year of his reign. ¹⁷ Now the king was attracted to Esther more than to any of the other women, and she won his favor and approval more than any of the other virgins. So he set a royal crown on her head and made her queen instead of Vashti. ¹⁸ And the king gave a great banquet, Esther's banquet, for all his nobles and officials. He proclaimed a holiday throughout the provinces and distributed gifts with royal liberality. ¹⁹ When the virgins were assembled a second time, Mordecai was sitting at the king's gate. ²⁰ But Esther had kept secret her family background and nationality just as Mordecai had told her to do, for she continued to follow Mordecai's instructions as she had done when he was bringing her up.

Esther 4:1-17

When Mordecai learned of all that had been done, he tore his clothes, put on sackcloth and ashes, and went out into the city, wailing loudly and bitterly. ² But he went only as far as the king's gate, because no one clothed in sackcloth was allowed to enter it. ³ In every province to which the edict and order of the king came, there was great mourning among the Jews, with fasting, weeping and wailing. Many lay in sackcloth and ashes. [4] When Esther's eunuchs and female attendants came and told her about Mordecai, she was in great distress. She sent clothes for him to put on instead of his sackcloth, but he would not accept them. [5] Then Esther summoned Hathak, one of the king's eunuchs assigned to attend her, and ordered him to find out what was troubling Mordecai and why. [6] So Hathak went out to Mordecai in the open square of the city in front of the king's gate. [7] Mordecai told him everything that had happened to him, including the exact amount of money Haman had promised to pay into the royal treasury for the destruction of the Jews. [8] He also gave him a copy of the text of the edict for their annihilation, which had been published in Susa, to show to Esther and explain it to her, and he told him to instruct her to go into the king's presence to beg for mercy and plead with him for her people. [9] Hathak went back and reported to Esther what Mordecai had said. [10] Then she instructed him to say to Mordecai, [11] "All the king's officials and the people of the royal provinces know that for any man or woman who approaches the king in the inner court without being summoned the king has but one law: that they be put to death unless the king extends the gold scepter to them and spares their lives. But thirty days have passed since I was called to go to the king." [12] When Esther's words were reported to Mordecai, [13] he sent back this answer: "Do not think that because you are in the king's house you alone of all the Jews will escape. [14] For if you remain silent at this time, relief and deliverance for the Jews will arise from another place, but you and your father's family will perish. And who knows but that you have come to your royal position for such a time as this?" [15] Then Esther sent this reply to Mordecai: [16] "Go, gather together all the Jews who are in Susa, and fast for me. Do not eat or drink for three days, night or day. I and my attendants will fast as you do. When this is done, I will go to the king, even though it is against the law. And if I perish, I perish." [17] So Mordecai went away and carried out all of Esther's instructions.

Esther 5:1-9
On the third day Esther put on her royal robes and stood in the inner court of the palace, in front of the king's hall. The king was sitting on his royal throne in the hall, facing the entrance. [2] When he saw Queen Esther standing in the court, he was pleased with her

and held out to her the gold scepter that was in his hand. So Esther approached and touched the tip of the scepter. ³ Then the king asked, "What is it, Queen Esther? What is your request? Even up to half the kingdom, it will be given you." ⁴ "If it pleases the king," replied Esther, "let the king, together with Haman, come today to a banquet I have prepared for him." ⁵ "Bring Haman at once," the king said, "so that we may do what Esther asks." So the king and Haman went to the banquet Esther had prepared. ⁶ As they were drinking wine, the king again asked Esther, "Now what is your petition? It will be given you. And what is your request? Even up to half the kingdom, it will be granted." ⁷ Esther replied, "My petition and my request is this: ⁸ If the king regards me with favor and if it pleases the king to grant my petition and fulfill my request, let the king and Haman come tomorrow to the banquet I will prepare for them. Then I will answer the king's question."

Esther 7:1-8

So the king and Haman went to Queen Esther's banquet, ² and as they were drinking wine on the second day, the king again asked, "Queen Esther, what is your petition? It will be given you. What is your request? Even up to half the kingdom, it will be granted."

191

³ Then Queen Esther answered, "If I have found favor with you, Your Majesty, and if it pleases you, grant me my life—this is my petition. And spare my people—this is my request. ⁴ For I and my people have been sold to be destroyed, killed and annihilated. If we had merely been sold as male and female slaves, I would have kept quiet, because no such distress would justify disturbing the king." ⁵ King Xerxes asked Queen Esther, "Who is he? Where is he—the man who has dared to do such a thing?" ⁶ Esther said, "An adversary and enemy! This vile Haman!" Then Haman was terrified before the king and queen. ⁷ The king got up in a rage, left his wine and went out into the palace garden. But Haman, realizing that the king had already decided his fate, stayed behind to beg Queen Esther for his life. ⁸ Just as the king returned from the palace garden to the banquet hall, Haman was falling on the couch where Esther was reclining. The king exclaimed, "Will he even molest the queen while she is with me in the house?"

Queen Esther was a woman who understood that her life had meaning and purpose. She was a woman who was willing to take a leap of faith to walk in the fullness of who God called her to be.

Even in the midst of an unstable current situation her faith was big enough to still surrender to God in order to be used by God.

Her Leadership: Servant Leadership

Servant leadership is a deeper level of transformational leadership. Servant leaders transform as they are being transformed by God. According to Rodin (2010) servant leaders are men and women who bring their purpose, passion, and character to their leadership style. When combined with their God-given skills and abilities for leadership, they bring out the best in people. Servant leadership is being in covenant with God in all areas in life. The word servant is about honoring God while the word leadership is about leading God's people. For the servant leader, God is everywhere and part of every aspect of life. Leadership from the perspective of a person who serves God is different than a person who does not. God is the driving force behind all servant leaders which in turn makes them better stewards over who God has called them to be. According to Greenleaf (2013), the servant-leader is a servant first. It begins with the natural feeling that one wants to serve first. Then conscious choice brings one to aspire to lead. That person is sharply different from one who is a leader first, perhaps because of the need to assuage an unusual power drive or to acquire material possessions. Queen Esther was a servant first then a leader. She had no idea what God was calling her to. What she did know is that she needed to remain open to whatever plans God had in store for her.

Queen Esther yielded to God's plan for her life and remained humble as she was elevated beyond her wildest dreams. According to Flint, Jr. (2012) the more successful and powerful you become (the world's view of success), the more difficult it becomes to remain the person who started out on that journey of servant leadership. The battlefield is littered with fallen business, spiritual, and political leaders, who started out with the right motives, but let selfishness take control of their lives. Servant Leadership calls for us to walk a fine line between who we are in God and who other people perceive us to be. It becomes a challenge for leadership who are sold out to God to remain humble enough to not take God's glory for who they are becoming. Leaders become almost superstars and public figures for some people. Servant leaders are intentional about making sure that God gets the credit for who they are becoming and that is exactly what Queen Esther did.

Your Lesson: Be a Surrendered Woman

What does it really mean to surrender to God? How do I give up who I wish I was to rest in who I really am? When do I walk away from the lie that I have created for my life and embrace all of who God called me to be as a leader? Who says that I have to be fake and like it? Where do I go now that I have to face my new truth? All of these questions and many more have altered the lives of many women. Some of us have lived for years uncomfortably comfortable in the lies of our lives. My sister, it is time to surrender everything that is not like God to God so that you can be healed and whole. A surrendered woman walks with the assurance that even in her fears about life, love, and leadership God has ordered her steps and has a plan for her that will blow her mind. Surrendered women are obedient to God's voice even when it makes little to no sense in the moment. Queen Esther heard God's voice to call a fast and do what no one has ever done before her.

Spiritual Position of Attention

Expansion of a Leader

DON'T LET YOUR GIFT TAKE YOU WHERE YOUR CHARACTER WON'T KEEP YOU

With what should I enter the Lord's presence? With what should I bow before the sovereign God? Should I enter his presence with burnt offerings, with year-old calves? Will the Lord accept a thousand rams, or ten thousand streams of olive oil? Should I give him my firstborn child as payment for my rebellion, my offspring-my own flesh and blood-for my sin? He has told you, O man, what is good, and what the Lord really wants from you; He wants you to promote justice, to be faithful, and to live obediently before your God. Micah 6:6-8 (NET)

Peace from God:_____
_____
_____
_____
_____
_____

My rest in God:_____
_____
_____
_____
_____
_____

My "yes" to God:_____

_____

_____

_____

_____

_____

Chapter Eight

Principle #7   Humble Submission

29 "Many daughters have done well, But you excel them all."

There comes a time in every woman's life where she must look herself in the mirror and face her truth. You can spend many years trying to be someone you were never meant to be. What happens when you look in the mirror and do not like what you see? Life changes for you when you submit your will to God's will in a humble way. Principle # 7 is Humble Submission. It is in this place of humble submission where you excel to be the woman God called you to be. This principle will be illuminated through Prophet Miriam. She is a powerful woman who demonstrated situational leadership.

The Lady: Prophet Miriam

Miriam is referred to fourteen times in the Old Testament. Although the name only appears a few times the places where it appears speaks volumes about her and what she left behind for women everywhere to look to as an example of a powerful leader. Miriam first appears as the unnamed sister of Moses in Exodus chapter two. Miriam is the first woman to be given the feminine word for Prophet. Her story appears in Exodus 2, Exodus 15, Numbers 12, Numbers 20, Numbers 26, Deuteronomy 24, I Chronicles 6, and Micah 6.

Exodus 2

Now a man from the house of Levi went and married a daughter of Levi. [2] The woman conceived and bore a son; and when she saw that he was beautiful, she hid him for three months. [3] But when she could hide him no longer, she got him a wicker basket and covered it over with tar and pitch. Then she put the child into it and set *it* among the reeds by the bank of the Nile. [4] His sister stood at a distance to find out what would happen to him. [5] The daughter of Pharaoh came down to bathe at the Nile, with her maidens walking alongside the Nile; and she saw the basket among the reeds and sent her maid, and she brought it *to her*.[6] When she opened *it*, she saw the child, and behold, *the* boy was crying. And she had pity on him and said, "This is one of the Hebrews' children." ⁷ Then his sister said to Pharaoh's daughter, "Shall I go and call a nurse for you from the Hebrew women that she may nurse the child for you?" ⁸ Pharaoh's daughter said to her, "Go *ahead*." So the girl went and called the child's mother. ⁹ Then Pharaoh's daughter said to her, "Take this child away and nurse him for me and I will give *you* your wages." So the woman took the child and nursed him. ¹⁰ The child grew, and she brought him to Pharaoh's daughter and he became her son. And she named him Moses, and said, "Because I drew him out of the water."

Exodus 15

²⁰ Miriam the prophetess, Aaron's sister, took the timbrel in her hand, and all the women went out after her with timbrels and with dancing. ²¹ Miriam answered them, "Sing to the LORD, for He is highly exalted; The horse and his rider He has hurled into the sea."

Numbers 12

Then Miriam and Aaron spoke against Moses because of the Cushite woman whom he had married (for he had married a Cushite woman); ² and they said, "Has the LORD indeed spoken only through Moses? Has He not spoken through us as well?" And the LORD heard it. ³ (Now the man Moses was very humble, more than any man who was on the face of the earth.) ⁴ Suddenly the LORD said to Moses and Aaron and to Miriam, "You three come out to the tent of meeting." So the three of them came out. ⁵ Then the LORD came down in a pillar of cloud and stood at the doorway of the tent, and He called Aaron and Miriam. When they had both come forward, ⁶ He said, "Hear now My words: If there is a prophet among you, I, the LORD, shall make Myself known to him in a vision. I shall speak with him in a dream. ⁷ "Not so, with My servant Moses, He is faithful in all My household; ⁸ With him I speak mouth to mouth, Even openly, and not in dark sayings, And he beholds the form of the LORD. Why then were you not afraid to speak against My servant, against Moses?" ⁹ So the anger of the LORD burned against them and He departed.¹⁰ But when the cloud had withdrawn from over the tent, behold, Miriam *was* leprous, as *white as* snow. As Aaron turned toward Miriam, behold, she *was* leprous. ¹¹ Then Aaron said to Moses, "Oh, my lord, I beg you, do not account *this* sin to us, in which we have acted foolishly and in which we have sinned. ¹² Oh, do not let her be like one dead, whose flesh is half eaten away

– -–

when he comes from his mother's womb!" [13] Moses cried out to the LORD, saying, "O God, heal her, I pray!" [14] But the LORD said to Moses, "If her father had but spit in her face, would she not bear her shame for seven days? Let her be shut up for seven days outside the camp, and afterward she may be received again." [15] So Miriam was shut up outside the camp for seven days, and the people did not move on until Miriam was received again. [16] Afterward, however, the people moved out from Hazeroth and camped in the wilderness of Paran.

Numbers 20:1
Then the sons of Israel, the whole congregation, came to the wilderness of Zin in the first month; and the people stayed at Kadesh. Now Miriam died there and was buried there.

Numbers 26
[59] The name of Amram's wife was Jochebed, the daughter of Levi, who was born to Levi in Egypt; and she bore to Amram: Aaron and Moses and their sister Miriam.

Deuteronomy 24
[8] "Be careful against an infection of leprosy, that you diligently observe and do according to all that the Levitical priests teach you; as I have commanded them, so you shall be careful to

do.[9] Remember what the LORD your God did to Miriam on the way as you came out of Egypt.

1 Chronicles 6

The sons of Levi were Gershon, Kohath and Merari. [2] The sons of Kohath were Amram, Izhar, Hebron and Uzziel. [3] The children of Amram were Aaron, Moses and Miriam.

Micah 6:4

"Indeed, I brought you up from the land of Egypt and ransomed you from the house of slavery, And I sent before you Moses, Aaron and Miriam.

The Bible gives us three portraits of Miriam: one as a young girl in Exodus 2, one as a young woman in Exodus 15, and one as a wise older woman in Numbers 12. She is a powerful woman who evolved over the course of her life. The Old Testament makes it clear that Miriam is a prophet, musician, praise dancer, and leader. Many women in the Bible serve in leadership roles yet they are not given credit for it. God gives Miriam the same honor of leadership as Aaron and Moses in Micah 6. The Bible speaks to her powerful leadership through the three snippets that we see of her. In Exodus 2 she led the charge in watching over her brother and engaging the

Princess to orchestrate her mother's reunion with Moses. Numbers 12 is where we see her chastisement from God for questioning how God chooses to use Moses. I often wonder why she was punished with leprosy and Aaron was not. What we can see clearly is that God took the time to speak to her directly. Leaders do not know everything and must submit to God for true guidance and correction when necessary. God confirmed that Miriam was sent to lead along with her brothers in Micah 6:4. Numbers 12 affirms how the people of Israel honored her leadership as they would not move until Miriam was healed.

Her Leadership: Situational Leadership

Miriam demonstrated a level of leadership that surpassed any attempt to silence her. When she was a young girl, when she was a young woman, and when she was an older woman her ability to speak set her apart. She had a situational approach to leadership. According to Hersey & Blanchard (2014) situational leadership is based on an interplay among: (1) the amount of guidance and direction (task behavior) a leader gives, (2) the amount of socioemotional support (relationship behavior) a leader provides, and (3) the readiness level that followers exhibit in performing a specific task, function or objective. Situational leaders change the style of leadership by observing specific characteristics and behaviors in order to maximize the leading objective. Miriam was a situational leader because the environment created a constant learning process. The three contextual places where Miriam appears in the Bible are very different. Miriam's situation in Exodus 2 called for a readiness level of the other women to effectively lead a movement to save her brother Moses. Miriam's situation in Exodus 15 was giving guidance and direction to the children of Israel as they celebrated their deliverance. Miriam's situation in Numbers 12 called for the socioemotional support that she provided to those that she led even while going through her own public humiliation. The mere fact that Miriam's death was chronicled in the Bible speaks volumes about how the people perceived her leadership.

Hersey, & Blanchard (2014) explain in *Management of Organizational Behavior: Leading Human Resources*, there is no one best way to influence people but a combination of ways. Miriam understood that she needed a mixed methodology of leadership styles within her leadership structure. A situational leadership approach provides for better outcomes especially as women maneuver through the ebb and flow of a social construct that gives them credibility in association with the men in their lives. Miriam was unnamed when she was brought on the scene in Exodus 2 yet she rose to a place of honor due to her leadership by the time she died in Numbers 20.

Your Lesson: Be a Powerful Woman

The best way for a woman to excel in who God called her to be is to take control over the negative thoughts that come to tell her to be quiet. Society and the church foster an environment where women feel intimidated and bullied into minimizing who they are. Powerful women accentuate the best of who they are, cultivate their growing edges, and collaborate with God as they continue growing. It takes internal strength to see the best in yourself when external forces continuously come up against you. The best of who you are will keep you while you cultivate your growing edges. My sisters, the truth hurts sometimes. You must be willing to be honest with yourself and open with God and admit where you need to become better. McKenzie (2002) says:

> Being open to God is not limiting God with your own preconceived notions or your idea of the future. Being open to God is not shackling God with what you want, how you feel, where you want to be, and what you deserve to doing right now. It is giving God a blank check and letting the Divine fill it in, trusting Him not to take more than necessary. Being open is telling God "I trust you with who I am and everything that I have." It is removing yourself from the control panel of your life, letting God drive and not limiting God or putting God in your own narrow box.

Maybe you are an excellent speaker but you are too defensive when people try to give you feedback. Maybe you are an excellent organizer but nobody can stand being near you because you are arrogant. Maybe you are kind on the surface but you expect everyone to tell you how great you are. Your growing edges are yours to work on. It is not up to everyone else to just deal with it. Finally, your prayer time, fasting, and study is how you collaborate with God as you grow. You cannot expect to grow in God if you never spend time with God. Talking to God without listening to God is pointless. Your desire to be a powerful woman comes with sacrifice. Miriam's life was powerful and exemplary of how God can and will use women.

Spiritual Position of Attention

Examination of a Leader

GOD CALLED YOU…WALK IN IT

This letter is from John, the elder. I am writing to the chosen lady and to her children, whom I love in the truth—as does everyone else who knows the truth— 2 John 1:1 (NLT)

Peace from God:_____
_____
_____
_____
_____
_____

My rest in God:_____
_____
_____
_____
_____
_____

My "yes" to God:_____
_____
_____
_____
_____
_____

Chapter Nine

Principle #8
Eternal Gratefulness

30 Charm is deceitful and beauty is passing, But a woman who fears the Lord, she shall be praised.

The essence of who you are is love. God is Love Spirit and we are created in the image of likeness of God's Spirit. When love is the driving force of your existence gratefulness is your vehicle. When you live in the space and grace of gratefulness you love people better, live a fuller life, and lead from a place of humility and excellence. Your faith takes you to a new level of service because you are fully yielded to God's will for your life. Principle # 8 is Eternal Gratefulness. This principle will be illuminated through Prophet Deborah. She is a woman of great faith who demonstrated steward leadership.

The Lady: Prophet Deborah

Prophet Deborah was the fourth and only woman judge. She was a leader and a warrior. She rose to leadership after Israel had been severely oppressed for twenty years. Unlike many women leaders in the Bible, she actually speaks. She is the only woman in the biblical narrative that is given the absolute credit for leading in the fullness of who she is. Her story is found in Judges 4 and 5.

Judges 4:4-14

[4] Now Deborah, a prophet, the wife of Lappidoth, was leading Israel at that time. [5] She held court under the Palm of Deborah between Ramah and Bethel in the hill country of Ephraim, and the Israelites went up to her to have their disputes decided. [6] She sent for Barak son of Abinoam from Kedesh in Naphtali and said to him, "The LORD, the God of Israel, commands you: 'Go, take with you ten thousand men of Naphtali and Zebulun and lead them up to Mount Tabor. [7] I will lead Sisera, the commander of Jabin's army, with his chariots and his troops to the Kishon River and give him into your hands.'" [8] Barak said to her, "If you go with me, I will go; but if you don't go with me, I won't go." [9] "Certainly I will go with you," said Deborah. "But because of the course you are taking, the honor will not be yours, for the LORD will deliver Sisera into the hands of a woman." So Deborah went with Barak to Kedesh. [10] There Barak summoned Zebulun and Naphtali, and ten thousand men went up

under his command. Deborah also went up with him. Now Heber the Kenite had separated himself from the Kenites, from the sons of Hobab the father-in-law of Moses, and had pitched his tent as far away as the oak in Zaanannim, which is near Kedesh. [12] Then they told Sisera that Barak the son of Abinoam had gone up to Mount Tabor. [13] Sisera called together all his chariots, nine hundred iron chariots, and all the people who were with him, from Harosheth-hagoyim to the river Kishon. [14] Deborah said to Barak, Arise for this day in which the Lord has given Sisera into your hand; behold, the Lord has gone out before you." So Barak went down from Mount Tabor with ten thousand men following him.

Judges 5
Then Deborah and Barak the son of Abinoam sang on that day, saying, [2] "That the leaders led in Israel, That the people volunteered, Bless the LORD! [3] "Hear, O kings; give ear, O rulers! I—to the LORD, I will sing, I will sing praise to the LORD, the God of Israel.[4] "LORD, when You went out from Seir, When You marched from the field of Edom, The earth quaked, the heavens also dripped, Even the clouds dripped water. The mountains quaked at the presence of the LORD, This Sinai, at the presence of

the LORD, the God of Israel. [6] "In the days of Shamgar the son of Anath, In the days of Jael, the highways were deserted, And travelers went by roundabout ways. [7] "The peasantry ceased, they ceased in Israel, Until I, Deborah, arose, Until I arose, a mother in Israel. [8] "New gods were chosen; Then war was in the gates. Not a shield or a spear was seen among forty thousand in Israel. [9] "My heart goes out to the commanders of Israel, The volunteers among the people; Bless the LORD! [10] "You who ride on white donkeys, You who sit on rich carpets, And you who travel on the road— sing! [11] "At the sound of those who divide flocks among the watering places, there they shall recount the righteous deeds of the LORD, The righteous deeds for His peasantry in Israel. Then the people of the LORD went down to the gates. [12] "Awake, awake, Deborah; Awake, awake, sing a song! Arise, Barak, and take away your captives, O son of Abinoam. [13] "Then survivors came down to the nobles; The people of the LORD came down to me as warriors. [14] "From Ephraim those whose root is in Amalek came down, Following you, Benjamin, with your peoples; From Machir commanders came down, And from Zebulun those who wield the staff of office. [15] "And the princes of Issachar were with Deborah

- - -

as was Issachar, so was Barak; Into the valley they rushed at his heels; Among the divisions of Reuben there were great resolves of heart. ¹⁶ "Why did you sit among the sheepfolds, To hear the piping for the flocks? Among the divisions of Reuben there were great searchings of heart. ¹⁷ "Gilead remained across the Jordan; and why did Dan stay in ships? Asher sat at the seashore, and remained by its landings. ¹⁸ "Zebulun was a people who despised their lives even to death, And Naphtali also, on the high places of the field. ¹⁹ "The kings came and fought; then fought the kings of Canaan At Taanach near the waters of Megiddo; They took no plunder in silver. ²⁰ "The stars fought from heaven, from their courses they fought against Sisera. ²¹ "The torrent of Kishon swept them away, the ancient torrent, the torrent Kishon. O my soul, march on with strength. ²² "Then the horses' hoofs beat from the dashing, the dashing of his valiant steeds. ²³ 'Curse Meroz,' said the angel of the LORD, 'Utterly curse its inhabitants; because they did not come to the help of the LORD, to the help of the LORD against the warriors.' ²⁴ "Most blessed of women is Jael, The wife of Heber the Kenite; Most blessed is she of women in the tent. ²⁵ "He asked for water and she gave him milk; In a magnificent bowl she brought him curds. **26** "She reached out her hand for the tent peg, and her right hand for the workmen's hammer. Then she struck Sisera, she smashed his head; and she shattered and pierced his temple. **27** "Between her feet he bowed, he fell, he lay; Between her feet he bowed, he fell; Where he bowed, there he fell dead. **28** "Out of the window she looked and lamented, the mother of Sisera through the lattice, 'Why does his chariot delay in coming? Why do the hoofbeats of his chariots tarry?' **29** "Her wise princesses would answer her, Indeed she repeats her words to herself, **30** 'Are they not finding, are they not dividing the spoil? A maiden, two maidens for every warrior; To Sisera a spoil of dyed work, A spoil of dyed work embroidered, Dyed work of double embroidery on the neck of the spoiler?' **31** "Thus let all Your enemies perish, O LORD; But let those who love Him be like the rising of the sun in its might." And the land was undisturbed for forty years.

Deborah was a woman of great faith who knew that God called her to greatness. She relied completely on God to lead, guide, and direct her. Although the Bible never describes her outward appearance, it is evident by the honor the people bestowed upon her that she was beautiful on the inside. Spiritual Alpha Females are intentional about being beautiful on the inside. It is in an internal space of gratefulness that women release the external forces that have held them hostage. It takes strength, self-assurance, and solid faith to be the first woman to be or do anything. Deborah was the first and only woman judge. She had no woman to model her leadership after and had every woman to blaze a trail of leadership for. Deborah had the grace and the grit to lead.

Her Leadership: Steward Leadership

Steward Leadership is contextual in that it calls on your authentic self to line up with who you see yourself growing to become. Your desire to manage yourself becomes your driving force. It is your ultimate desire to honor God by being a good steward over yourself. For those who believe in following God's voice and vision for their lives the transformation from being self-driven to being God-driven is the key to becoming a godly steward. Prophet Deborah yielded to the voice of God in the face of being the only woman in her position. I can just imagine the looks that she received, the condescending tone she endured, and the dismissive attitudes she managed to overcome as she led God's people under God's anointing. Being a true godly steward requires consistent intentional self- reflection because the "who" of steward leader serves as a reflection of the "who' of God. Leading from a place of eternal gratefulness allows for the ebb and flow of dealing with the various struggles in growing as a woman leader. According to Chissiter (2012):

> Struggle changes us; it grows us up. It takes the dew off the rose and gilt off the silver. It turns the fantasies of life into reality. But struggle does more than that. It also give life depth and vision, insight and understanding, compassion and character. It not only transforms us, it makes us transforming as well. Then we become equal to the pressures of the world around us. Once we have truly struggled with something that stretches the elastic of the spirit, we are worthy to walk with others in the struggle too.

Prophet Deborah walked in the grace of God as change and struggle was happening all around her. She was a fierce warrior woman which was contrary to the "stay in your place" role that the average woman of her time was subjected to. She was a prophetic woman who used her voice to share God's messages living in a time when women were seen and not heard.

Steward leadership is a concept that calls on an inner discipline that allows your spirit to yield to the transformative power of God in all aspects of your life. According to Rodin (2010) the theory of steward leadership states:

First, these theories start with acts of leadership deemed to be effective and try to work back to find common traits and characteristics. Second, they rely on the basic goodness of human nature as the basis for the work of leadership. And third, they have a common view that the leader moves people toward the goal of personal happiness with the hope and belief that people—and leaders——can know what makes them happy and can pursue it without harming their neighbor. The steward leader approach is based on the transformation that takes place in the heart of the leader as a faithful and godly steward, and works from this inner transformation (which is ongoing) to the outward impact when a godly steward is called to lead. This inward-outward direction and the emphasis of being over doing set the steward leader apart from this array of secular leadership theories.

Steward leadership is a challenge for those who have spent most of their time focusing on the external results of leadership and paying little attention to the internal aspects of leadership. One of the hardest places to remain humble is in the influence and the power we hold over people and decisions. Prophet Deborah was in a leadership role where her influence and power was extensive. It was in the recognition of that power and influence that kept her in a place of eternal gratefulness. There is nothing wrong with having power and influence unless you use it to marginalize people.

We are first stewards over who we are and then stewards over our Kingdom assignment. There are two kingdoms competing for our loyalty: God's and Satan's. According to Rodin (2010):

The fight is about our perception of grace. In God's Kingdom grace is unmerited, underserved, and unlimited. In Satan's kingdom grace is confined and conditional. When it comes to grace the enemy, however, distorts the free response of grace into a duty that we must carry out in allegiance to God. When our response to grace becomes an obligation, we are again thrown back on ourselves to perform. This is burdensome and robs us of the joy of the obedient steward. But it is much more heinous than that. In turning gracious response into burdensome duty, the enemy has also put us in control of our relationship with God. And with control comes a sense of ownership. Once we believe that we control our relationship with God, we have been had. We begin to worship out of guilt. We become legalistic about our devotional time. When we read scripture, we do it impatiently, always looking for a key verse that we can use productively. Gone is the joy of worship, the intimacy of devotional time in the presence of the spirit and the meditation on Scripture just for the sake of communing with the Word of God.

There is great danger in being loyal to the wrong kingdom. The test in the testimony is can you hold on to what you know to be the truth of God in the midst of the lies of the enemy. Stewardship calls us to be the caretaker of God's most precious gift, us. Who I am as a leader and what I do as a leader must line up. Prophet Deborah lived a balanced life where who she was lined up with what she did.

Your Lesson: Be A Woman of Great Faith

Is faith a noun or is faith a verb? I often wonder if faith is in a category all by itself. I say that because you never hear people say, "I am faithing it" and then there is great debate about whether faith is a place or a thing. Being a woman of great faith puts you in a category all by yourself. You have the grit to stand in the face of the impossible without flinching and you have the grace to speak your truth in a place that tells you to be quiet. Your eternally grateful spirit allows the love on the inside to reflect on the outside. People that you would never even imagine honor who you are and what you do because you are authentically in love with God. Prophet Deborah was praised because God anointed her and she walked, talked, and led under that anointing. Being a woman of faith requires you to embrace the anointing on your life and cultivate it so that you can be the best you that you can be. What is the point of God showering you with all that anointing if you are not going to use it to be a blessing to the Kingdom? Spiritual Alpha Females love God with every fiber of their being and are eternally grateful for everything God has brought them through and to.

Spiritual Position of Attention

Expectation of a Leader

WALK IN THE FULLNESS OF WHO YOU ARE

When I look up at the heavens, which your fingers made, and see the moon and the stars, which you set in place, of what importance is the human race, that you should notice them? Of what importance is mankind, that you should pay attention to them, and make them a little less than the heavenly beings? You grant mankind honor and majesty; you appoint them to rule over your creation; you have placed everything under their authority, including all the sheep and cattle, as well as the wild animals, the birds in the sky, the fish in the sea and everything that moves through the currents of the sea. Psalm 8:3-8 (NET)

Peace from God:_____

_____

_____

_____

_____

_____

My rest in God:_____

_____

_____

_____

_____

_____

My "yes" to God:_____

_____

_____

_____

_____

_____

Chapter Ten

Principle #9

Daughter of the Queen

31 Give her of the fruit of her hands, And let her own works praise her in the gates.

Who are you? What do you want? What has God called you to? What/Who causes you to shrink back into the fakeness of who you are? What/Who keeps you from standing in the fullness of who you are? All of these questions are worth asking however if you do not get the answers to them your life will continue to be limited. There is a place in God where you walk taller, speak louder, and live fuller. That place is authentic, that place is peaceful, that place feels like home. We talk a lot about being a child of the King and we never talk about being the Daughter of the Queen. Genesis says that *They* (male and female) created humankind in *Their* image and in *Their* likeness. Women were created in the image and likeness of *They*. When I think about what it means to honor God, I must honor the fullness of who God is as I understand it. The Queen is equal to the King. To say that I am a daughter of the King is also to say that

I am a daughter of the Queen. The Queen is our female divine reflection. All the feminine goodness that we were created in comes from the Queen. Our exceptional emotional intelligence, our ability to love unconditionally, our amazingly accurate intuition, our ability to master our intellect, our ability to multi-task, and so much more speak volumes about the good that we were created to bring to the not good. My beloved sisters, we can honor Her without dishonoring Him. Principle #9 is Daughter of the Queen. This principle will be illuminated through you. You are a woman who honors God and you demonstrate spiritual alpha leadership.

The Lady: You

You are an amazing woman with great potential. Over the course of your life you have experienced some highs and lows. You have managed to hold on even when your feet were swinging in the wind. What gives you so much strength? Who do you see when you look in the mirror? Whose voice do you hear when the noise of life is quiet? The religious community and society has taught us that the maleness of God is sacred. There is no room for the femaleness of

God even though the first book of the Bible speaks of her. What does that mean for women who want to honor God with the fullness of who they are? The progression of who you are becoming can be found in Genesis 2, Genesis 16, Judges 19, Isaiah 52, Jeremiah 8, Joel 2, Malachi 2, 1 Corinthians 11, and 2 Corinthians 4.

Genesis 2:18-22 (NLT)

Then the LORD God said, "It is not good for the man to be alone. I will make a helper who is just right for him." [19] So the LORD God formed from the ground all the wild animals and all the birds of the sky. He brought them to the man to see what he would call them, and the man chose a name for each one. [20] He gave names to all the livestock, all the birds of the sky, and all the wild animals. But still there was no helper just right for him. [21] So the LORD God caused the man to fall into a deep sleep. While the man slept,
the LORD God took out one of the man's ribs and closed up the opening. [22] Then the LORD God made a woman from the rib, and he brought her to the man.

Genesis 16 (NLT)

Now Sarai, Abram's wife, had not given birth to any children, but she had an Egyptian servant named Hagar. [2] So Sarai said to Abram,

"Since the LORD has prevented me from having children, have sexual relations with my servant. Perhaps I can have a family by her." Abram did what Sarai told him. ³ So after Abram had lived in Canaan for ten years, Sarai, Abram's wife, gave Hagar, her Egyptian servant, to her husband to be his wife. ⁴ He had sexual relations with Hagar, and she became pregnant. Once Hagar realized she was pregnant, she despised Sarai. ⁵ Then Sarai said to Abram, "You have brought this wrong on me! I allowed my servant to have sexual relations with you, but when she realized that she was pregnant, she despised me. May the LORD judge between you and me!" ⁶ Abram said to Sarai, "Since your servant is under your authority, do to her whatever you think best." Then Sarai treated Hagar harshly, so she ran away from Sarai. ⁷ The LORD's angel found Hagar near a spring of water in the desert—the spring that is along the road to Shur. ⁸ He said, "Hagar, servant of Sarai, where have you come from, and where are you going?" She replied, "I'm running away from my mistress, Sarai." ⁹ Then the LORD's angel said to her, "Return to your mistress and submit to her authority. ¹⁰ I will greatly multiply your descendants," the LORD's angel added, "so that they will be too numerous to count." ¹¹ Then the LORD's angel said to her, "You are

---

now pregnant and are about to give birth to a son. You are to name him Ishmael, for the LORD has heard your painful groans. ¹² He will be a wild donkey of a man. He will be hostile to everyone, and everyone will be hostile to him. He will live away from his brothers." ¹³ So Hagar named the LORD who spoke to her, "You are the God who sees me," for she said, "Here I have seen one who sees me!" ¹⁴ That is why the well was called Beer Lahai Roi. (It is located between Kadesh and Bered.) ¹⁵ So Hagar gave birth to Abram's son, whom Abram named Ishmael. ¹⁶ (Now Abram was 86 years old when Hagar gave birth to Ishmael.)

Judges 19 (NET)

In those days Israel had no king. There was a Levite living temporarily in the remote region of the Ephraimite hill country. He acquired a concubine from Bethlehem in Judah. ² However, she got angry at him and went home to her father's house in Bethlehem in Judah. When she had been there four months, ³ her husband came after her, hoping he could convince her to return. He brought with him his servant and a pair of donkeys. When she brought him into her father's house and the girl's father saw him, he greeted him warmly. ⁴ His father-in-law, the girl's father, persuaded him to stay

---

with him for three days, and they ate and drank together, and spent the night there. ⁵ On the fourth day they woke up early and the Levite got ready to leave. But the girl's father said to his son-in-law, "Have a bite to eat for some energy, then you can go." ⁶ So the two of them sat down and had a meal together. Then the girl's father said to the man, "Why not stay another night and have a good time!" ⁷ When the man got ready to leave, his father-in-law convinced him to stay another night. ⁸ He woke up early in the morning on the fifth day so he could leave, but the girl's father said, "Get some energy. Wait until later in the day to leave!" So they ate a meal together. ⁹ When the man got ready to leave with his concubine and his servant, his father-in-law, the girl's father, said to him, "Look! The day is almost over! Stay another night! Since the day is over, stay another night here and have a good time. You can get up early tomorrow and start your trip home." ¹⁰ But the man did not want to stay another night. He left and traveled as far as Jebus (that is, Jerusalem). He had with him a pair of saddled donkeys and his concubine. ¹¹ When they got near Jebus, it was getting quite late and the servant said to his master, "Come on, let's stop at this Jebusite city and spend the night in it." ¹² But his master said to him, "We should not stop at a foreign city where non-Israelites live. We will travel on to Gibeah." [13] He said to his servant, "Come on, we will go into one of the other towns and spend the night in Gibeah or Ramah." [14] So they traveled on, and the sun went down when they were near Gibeah in the territory of Benjamin. [15] They stopped there and decided to spend the night in Gibeah. They came into the city and sat down in the town square, but no one invited them to spend the night. [16] But then an old man passed by, returning at the end of the day from his work in the field. The man was from the Ephraimite hill country; he was living temporarily in Gibeah. (The residents of the town were Benjaminites.) [17] When he looked up and saw the traveler in the town square, the old man said, "Where are you heading? Where do you come from?" [18] The Levite said to him, "We are traveling from Bethlehem in Judah to the remote region of the Ephraimite hill country. That's where I'm from. I had business in Bethlehem in Judah, but now I'm heading home. But no one has invited me into their home. [19] We have enough straw and grain for our donkeys, and there is enough food and wine for me, your female servant, and the young man who is with your servants. We lack nothing." [20] The old man said, "Everything is just fine! I will take care of all your needs.

--‑

But don't spend the night in the town square." ²¹ So he brought him to his house and fed the donkeys. They washed their feet and had a meal. ²² They were having a good time, when suddenly some men of the city, some good-for-nothings, surrounded the house and kept beating on the door. They said to the old man who owned the house, "Send out the man who came to visit you so we can have sex with him." ²³ The man who owned the house went outside and said to them, "No, my brothers! Don't do this wicked thing! After all, this man is a guest in my house. Don't do such a disgraceful thing! ²⁴ Here are my virgin daughter and my guest's concubine. I will send them out and you can abuse them and do to them whatever you like. But don't do such a disgraceful thing to this man!" ²⁵ The men refused to listen to him, so the Levite grabbed his concubine and made her go outside. They raped her and abused her all night long until morning. They let her go at dawn. ²⁶ The woman arrived back at daybreak and was sprawled out on the doorstep of the house where her master was staying until it became light. ²⁷ When her master got up in the morning, opened the doors of the house, and went outside to start on his journey, there was the woman, his concubine, sprawled out on the doorstep of the house with her hands on the threshold. [28] He said to her, "Get up, let's leave!" But there was no response. He put her on the donkey and went home. [29] When he got home, he took a knife, grabbed his concubine, and carved her up into twelve pieces. Then he sent the pieces throughout Israel. [30] Everyone who saw the sight said, "Nothing like this has happened or been witnessed during the entire time since the Israelites left the land of Egypt! Take careful note of it! Discuss it and speak!"

Isaiah 52:1-3 (NLT)

Wake up, wake up, O Zion! Clothe yourself with strength. Put on your beautiful clothes, O holy city of Jerusalem, for unclean and godless people will enter your gates no longer. [2] Rise from the dust, O Jerusalem. Sit in a place of honor. Remove the chains of slavery from your neck, O captive daughter of Zion. [3] For this is what the LORD says: "When I sold you into exile, I received no payment. Now I can redeem you without having to pay for you."

Jeremiah 8:8-22 (NASB)

[8]" How can you say, 'We are wise and the law of the LORD is with us'? But behold, the lying pen of the scribes has made it into a lie. [9]"The wise men are put to shame, They are dismayed and caught;

Behold, they have rejected the word of the LORD, And what kind of wisdom do they have? ¹⁰"Therefore I will give their wives to others, their fields to new owners; Because from the least even to the greatest. Everyone is greedy for gain; From the prophet even to the priest. Everyone practices deceit. ¹¹"They heal the brokenness of the daughter of My people superficially, Saying, 'Peace, peace,' But there is no peace. ¹²"Were they ashamed because of the abomination they had done? They certainly were not ashamed, And they did not know how to blush; Therefore they shall fall among those who fall; At the time of their punishment they shall be brought down," Says the LORD. ¹³"I will surely snatch them away," declares the LORD; "There will be no grapes on the vine and no figs on the fig tree, and the leaf will wither; And what I have given them will pass away." ¹⁴Why are we sitting still? Assemble yourselves, and let us go into the fortified cities and let us perish there, because the LORD our God has doomed us and given us poisoned water to drink, For we have sinned against the LORD. ¹⁵We waited for peace, but no good came; for a time of healing, but behold, terror! ¹⁶From Dan is heard the snorting of his horses; at the sound of the neighing of his stallions the whole land quakes; For they come and devour the land and its fullness, The city and its inhabitants. [17]"For behold, I am sending serpents against you, Adders, for which there is no charm, And they will bite you," declares the LORD. [18]My sorrow is beyond healing, My heart is faint within me! [19]Behold, listen! The cry of the daughter of my people from a distant land: "Is the LORD not in Zion? Is her King not within her?" "Why have they provoked Me with their graven images, with foreign idols?" [20]"Harvest is past, summer is ended, And we are not saved." [21]For the brokenness of the daughter of my people I am broken; I mourn, dismay has taken hold of me. [22]Is there no balm in Gilead? Is there no physician there? Why then has not the health of the daughter of my people been restored?

Joel 2:12-32 (NET)

"Yet even now," the LORD says, "return to me with all your heart— with fasting, weeping, and mourning. Tear your hearts, not just your garments!" [13] Return to the LORD your God, for he is merciful and compassionate, slow to anger and boundless in loyal love—often relenting from calamitous punishment. [14] Who knows? Perhaps he will be compassionate and grant a reprieve, and leave blessing in his wake—a meal offering and a drink offering for you to offer to the Lord your God! **15** Blow the trumpet in Zion. Announce a holy fast; proclaim a sacred assembly! **16** Gather the people; sanctify an assembly! Gather the elders; gather the children and the nursing infants. Let the bridegroom come out from his bedroom and the bride from her private quarters. **17** Let the priests, those who serve the LORD, weep from the vestibule all the way back to the altar. Let them say, "Have pity, O LORD, on your people; please do not turn over your inheritance to be mocked, to become a proverb among the nations. Why should it be said among the peoples, "Where is their God?" **18** Then the LORD became zealous for his land; he had compassion on his people. **19** The LORD responded to his people, "Look! I am about to restore your grain as well as fresh wine and olive oil. You will be fully satisfied. I will never again make you an object of mockery among the nations. **20** I will remove the one from the north far from you. I will drive him out to a dry and desolate place. Those in front will be driven eastward into the Dead Sea, and those in back westward into the Mediterranean Sea. His stench will rise up as a foul smell." Indeed, the LORD has accomplished great things. **21** Do not fear, my land! Rejoice and be glad, because the LORD has accomplished great things! ²² Do not fear, wild animals! For the pastures of the wilderness are again green with grass. Indeed, the trees bear their fruit; the fig tree and the vine yield to their fullest. ²³ Citizens of Zion, rejoice! Be glad because of what the LORD your God has done! For he has given to you the early rains as vindication. He has sent to you the rains—both the early and the late rains as formerly. ²⁴ The threshing floors are full of grain; the vats overflow with fresh wine and olive oil. ²⁵ I will make up for the years that the *'arbeh*-locust consumed your crops— the *yeleq*-locust, the *hasil*-locust, and the *gazam*-locust— my great army that I sent against you. ²⁶ You will have plenty to eat ,and your hunger will be fully satisfied; you will praise the name of the LORD your God, who has acted wondrously in your behalf. My people will never again be put to shame. ²⁷ You will be convinced that I am in the midst of Israel. I am the LORD your God; there is no other. My people will never again be put to shame. ²⁸ After all of this I will pour out my Spirit on all kinds of people. Your sons and daughters will prophesy. Your elderly will have revelatory dreams; your young men will see prophetic visions. ²⁹ Even on male and female servants I will pour out my

Spirit in those days. [30] I will produce portents both in the sky and on the earth— blood, fire, and columns of smoke. [31] The sunlight will be turned to darkness and the moon to the color of blood, before the day of the Lord comes that great and terrible day! [32] It will so happen that everyone who calls on the name of the Lord will be delivered. For on Mount Zion and in Jerusalem there will be those who survive, just as the LORD has promised; the remnant will be those whom the LORD will call.

Malachi 2:1-16 (NET)

"Now, you priests, this commandment is for you. [2] If you do not listen and take seriously the need to honor my name," says the LORD who rules over all, "I will send judgment on you and turn your blessings into curses—indeed, I have already done so because you are not taking it to heart. [3] I am about to discipline your children and will spread offal on your faces, the very offal produced at your festivals, and you will be carried away along with it. [4] Then you will know that I sent this commandment to you so that my covenant may continue to be with Levi," says the LORD who rules over all. [5] "My covenant with him was designed to bring life and peace. I gave its statutes to him to fill him with awe, and he indeed revered me and stood in awe before me. ⁶ He taught what was true; sinful words were not found on his lips. He walked with me in peace and integrity, and he turned many people away from sin. ⁷ For the lips of a priest should preserve knowledge of sacred things, and people should seek instruction from him because he is the messenger of the LORD who rules over all. ⁸ You, however, have turned from the way. You have caused many to violate the law; you have corrupted the covenant with Levi," says the LORD who rules over all. ⁹ "Therefore, I have caused you to be ignored and belittled before all people to the extent to which you are not following after me and are showing partiality in your instruction." ¹⁰ Do we not all have one father? Did not one God create us? Why do we betray one another, in this way making light of the covenant of our ancestors? ¹¹ Judah has become disloyal, and unspeakable sins have been committed in Israel and Jerusalem. For Judah has profaned the holy things that the LORD loves and has turned to a foreign god! ¹² May the LORD cut off from the community of Jacob every last person who does this, as well as the person who presents improper offerings to the LORD who rules over all! ¹³ You also do this: You cover the altar of the LORD with tears as you weep and groan, because he no longer pays any attention to the offering nor accepts it favorably from you. ¹⁴ Yet you ask, "Why?" The LORD is testifying against you on behalf of the wife you married when you were young, to whom you have become unfaithful even though she is your companion and wife by law. ¹⁵ No one who has even a small portion of the Spirit in him does this. What did our ancestor do when seeking a child from God? Be attentive, then, to your own spirit, for one should not be disloyal to the wife he took in his youth. ¹⁶ "I hate divorce," says the LORD God of Israel, "and the one who is guilty of violence," says the LORD who rules over all. "Pay attention to your conscience, and do not be unfaithful."

1 Corinthians 11

I praise you because you remember me in everything and maintain the traditions just as I passed them on to you. ³ But I want you to know that Christ is the head of every man, and the man is the head of a woman, and God is the head of Christ. ⁴ Any man who prays or prophesies with his head covered disgraces his head. ⁵ But any woman who prays or prophesies with her head uncovered disgraces her head, for it is one and the same thing as having a shaved head. ⁶ For if a woman will not cover her head, she should cut off her hair. But if it is disgraceful for a woman to have her hair cut off or her head shaved, she should cover her head. [7] For a man should not have his head covered, since he is the image and glory of God. But the woman is the glory of the man. [8] For man did not come from woman, but woman from man. [9] Neither was man created for the sake of woman, but woman for man. [10] For this reason a woman should have a symbol of authority on her head, because of the angels. [11] In any case, in the Lord woman is not independent of man, nor is man independent of woman. [12] For just as woman came from man, so man comes through woman. But all things come from God. [13] Judge for yourselves: Is it proper for a woman to pray to God with her head uncovered? [14] Does not nature itself teach you that if a man has long hair, it is a disgrace for him, [15] but if a woman has long hair, it is her glory? For her hair is given to her for a covering. [16] If anyone intends to quarrel about this, we have no other practice, nor do the churches of God.

2 Corinthians 4:7-18 (MSG)

[7-12] If you only look at us, you might well miss the brightness. We carry this precious Message around in the unadorned clay pots of our ordinary lives. That's to prevent anyone from confusing God's

incomparable power with us. As it is, there's not much chance of that. You know for yourselves that we're not much to look at. We've been surrounded and battered by troubles, but we're not demoralized; we're not sure what to do, but we know that God knows what to do; we've been spiritually terrorized, but God hasn't left our side; we've been thrown down, but we haven't broken. What they did to Jesus, they do to us—trial and torture, mockery and murder; what Jesus did among them, he does in us—he lives! Our lives are at constant risk for Jesus' sake, which makes Jesus' life all the more evident in us. While we're going through the worst, you're getting in on the best! **13-15** We're not keeping this quiet, not on your life. Just like the psalmist who wrote, "I believed it, so I said it," we say what we believe. And what we believe is that the One who raised up the Master Jesus will just as certainly raise us up with you, alive. Every detail works to your advantage and to God's glory: more and more grace, more and more people, more and more praise! **16-18** So we're not giving up. How could we! Even though on the outside it often looks like things are falling apart on us, on the inside, where God is making new life, not a day goes by without his unfolding grace. These hard times are small potatoes compared to the coming good times, the lavish celebration prepared for us. There's far more here than meets the eye. The things we see now are here today, gone tomorrow. But the things we can't see now will last forever

The evolution of who you are is contextual to you. Growing into the woman God calls you to be is a process. Moving from the marginalizing framework that you have been taught to a more liberated framework takes time. Genesis 2, Genesis 16, Judges 19, Isaiah 52, Jeremiah 8, Joel 2, Malachi 2, 1 Corinthians 11, and 2 Corinthians 4 show a trajectory of how women have been presented in the Bible. Genesis 2 shares that you were created to make the not good, good. It was not good for the man to be alone, then there was her. She was created to bring goodness and purpose to his life. Genesis 16 shares Hagar's story. She was a young girl who was a servant to Sarai. She was given to Abram to have his baby. When Sarai got what she thought she wanted she turned on her. Sisterhood is about loyalty and this story shows the dysfunction that can occur in female relationships. Judges 19 shares a horrific story about the objectification of women. A woman who is never even given a name got angry with her husband and left him because he mistreated her. The concubine's husband pursued her at her father's house. The text never says she wanted to go back, however she did. The night before they left to go home, a mob came to have sex with him and he willingly, forcibly gave her over to the mob and they raped her all night long. She made it back to the doorstep and was left to die. Her husband took her dead body home, cut her up into twelve pieces and sent her body parts throughout the 12 tribes of Israel.

Isaiah 52 shares God's instruction for women to rise up and loose the chains that are around their necks. There is a place of honor that God desires to restore to women. Jeremiah 8 shares that God cares about your brokenness at the hands of religious men. Isaiah shares God's grief about your brokenness and affirmation that healing belongs to you. Joel 2 shares that God is intentional about pouring the Holy Spirit upon you. It was not by accident or happenstance that the anointing of God is on your life. Malachi 2 shares God's chastisement of men who are disloyal to their wives. It confirms and affirms that God created women and men in the same spirit. 1 Corinthians 11 shares the traumatic, marginalizing, restrictive dogma and doctrine that women have been held hostage to by the religious community. Finally, 2 Corinthians shares the many emotional, intellectual, physical, and spiritual hurdles that women have experienced. It shares your God ordained protection and victory. You have chosen to honor God with the fullness of who you are. All of the sadness, all of the brokenness, all of the questions, all of the affirmations, all of the successes, all of the joy that has sustained you through the good, bad, and the ugly has shaped you into the woman that you are. You are a survivor, you are an overcomer, you are a Daughter of the Queen.

Your Leadership: Spiritual Alpha Leadership

Leadership has been a hot topic for a long time. The church has been talking about it since the book of Genesis. The Bible shares many wonderful stories about leaders who are led by the Spirit as well as those who are not. Spiritual leaders as described by Sanders (2007) are those that are not elected, appointed, or created by synods or churchly assemblies. God alone makes a spiritual leader. Sanders suggestion makes it clear that for him the spiritual in leadership is a direct reflection of them being chosen by God. The Bible shares some leaders who were chosen by God yet they were not very spiritual after all was said and done. The Bible says in 1 Timothy

3:1 (NEB), "To aspire to leadership is an honorable ambition." With that being said those who aspire to be a leader have ambition that motivates them to be better. It seems to me that the spiritual component to leadership is more about the person's intentionality in their leadership. For me, spiritual leadership has everything to do our saying yes to God in relation to: Questions, language, drive, the work of the Holy Spirit, and improving.

The Question about Spiritual Leadership

There is great debate about whether a leader is born or created. I wonder what that means for all of the people who learned how to be a spiritual leader. I am not convinced that even the leaders in the Bible that God clearly called, were spiritual already. Sanders (2007) poses the question, is it not better for the position to seek out the person rather than the person to seek out the position? It reminds me of the selection of the new King after Saul was relinquished of his kingship. David had no idea that God had chosen him for the King position. He was a young man who followed his father's guidance and became an excellent sheep herder. The Bible never says anything about his leadership ability or his spirituality. What it does say is that he was the youngest and his father never even considered him when the Prophet Samuel came to him. God chose him based on what God knew he would become not based on who he was at that moment. It seems to me that God calls even when the person being called is not immediately ready. When God called Moses he was not ready so God sent Aaron with him. When God called Barak he was not ready so Prophet Deborah went with him. There are times when a person desires to lead yet they need someone to show them how to lead. In David's case once he volunteered to kill Goliath he spent a lot of time with King Saul learning how to lead. His spirituality developed over the course of his life.

Sanders also talks about his perception of leadership being God given where the person does not desire leadership. He lifts Jeremiah 45:5 that says, "Should you then seek great things for yourself? Seek them not." According to Sanders that ambition is problematic. It all comes down to whether their motivation is to please God or to please themselves. Sanders (2007) says desiring to excel is not a sin. It is motivation that determines ambition's character. Our Lord never taught against the urge to high achievement, but He did expose and condemn unworthy motivation.

251

From my perspective, spiritual leadership is an oxymoron if the person leading is not seeking God for everything. Sanders (2007) goes on to say:

> Leaders are needed who are authoritative, spiritual, and sacrificial. Authoritative because people desire reliable leaders who know where they are going and are confident of getting there. Spiritual, because without a strong relationship to God, even the most attractive and competent person cannot lead people to God. Sacrificial, because this trait follows the model of Jesus, who gave Himself for the whole world and who calls us to follow in His steps.

Spiritual leaders seek God for their guidance and direction. Whether God chooses them or they seek God to be chosen, they are spiritual leaders.

Language of Spiritual Leadership

Language matters. How you use language to describe leadership is a direct reflection on how you perceive the necessary components in leadership. Sanders (2007) raised the point that the King James Bible uses *leader* only six times while *servant* is used much more frequently. It seems to me that Sanders is making the point that the Bible leans toward calling leaders servants for a spiritual reason. The language that Sanders uses makes me believe that spiritual leadership is not something that people can attain. It seems like either God calls you or you remain a follower. Sanders goes on to raise two principles of leadership that Jesus raised in Mark 10:38-40: Sovereignty: To sit at my right or left is not for me grant in verse 40 and Suffering: Can you drink the cup I drink and be baptized with the baptism I am baptized with in verse 38 . The use of sovereign and suffering language leads me to believe that spiritual leadership requires a level of spiritual maturity that would take a lifetime to achieve. Spiritual maturity happens over the course of life experience. Regardless of what I think, Sanders (2007) says:

> Effective spiritual leadership does not come as a result of theological training or seminary degree, as important as education is. Jesus told His disciples, "You did not choose me, but I chose you and appointed you" (John 15:16). The sovereign selection of God gives great confidence to Christian workers. We can truly say, "I am here neither by

selection of an individual nor election of a group but by the almighty appointment of God.

The Drive of Spiritual Leadership

Leadership is something that is developed over time. Even the best of the best learn and grow as they lead. The driving force in leadership is the desire to be better leaders. According to Sanders (2007) spiritual leadership blends natural and spiritual qualities. It transcends the power of personality and all other natural gifts. The personality of the spiritual leader influences others because it is penetrated, saturated, and empowered by the Holy Spirit. As the leader gives control of their life to the Spirit the Spirit's power flows through them to others. Modeling spiritual leadership drives the growth and development of those being led as well as the one doing the leading. As I think about the modeling that I do in my life I am inspired by the good role models that I have had. Modeling intelligence, love, and leadership is what I strive to do. I cannot expect women to model what they do not see.

The various challenges of leadership help to make each leader unique. I say that because each challenge helps to develop the leader intellectually, emotionally, as well as spiritually. When I think about what it takes for me to model spiritual leadership, I am reminded that I have to be myself. According to Kouzes and Posner (2012) before you can become a credible leader-one who connects what you say with what you do-you first have to find your voice. To find your voice you have to explore your inner self. You have to discover what you care about, what defines you, and what makes you who you are. Spiritual leaders must know who they are. Unfortunately, many leaders are caught between who they want to be and who other people say they should be and for some that includes what they think God wants. I believe that true spiritual leadership keeps the person mindful that things change and they must rely on God to help them move through the changes that come. Spiritual leaders must embrace their personal change as well as help those that follow embrace the collective change that is inevitable.

Leadership involves forging change not forcing change. Dr. King did not force anyone to follow a non-violent philosophy or lifestyle. People followed Dr. King because his words lined up with his actions. His spirituality evolved as he continued to seek God in the face of being in the spotlight all the time. Kouzer and Posner

(2012) share that one of the toughest aspects of being a leader is that you're always onstage. People are always watching you, always talking about you, always testing your credibility. I willingly accepted a leadership position. In my acceptance came the realization that my life is now on display. Dr. King understood that his life was on display as well. A major component of spiritual leadership is presenting a positive credible image. As I continue to lead I remain aware that who I am and what I present is inextricably linked. Spirituality is contextual and so is leadership. What works in one situation may not work in another. There needs to be a significant level of flexibility that comes with spiritual leadership. Change happens and it is not easy for some people to accept. As a leader I accept that I have the profound responsibility of being a change agent that helps to transform the lives of the people that I lead. True spiritual leaders inspire people to move from where they are to where they dream of being as they watch the leader keep God first.

The Work of the Spirit in Leadership

To say that one is spiritual without being spirit-filled seems unimaginable. Spiritual leadership requires spirit filled people. Sanders lifts Acts 20:28 where it says, "Keep watch over yourselves and all the flock of which the Holy Spirit has made you overseers." The text suggests that the leader has a responsibility to keep watch over themselves prior to leading others. I like the personal accountability to God first and foremost. According to Sanders (2007) to be filled with the Spirit is to be controlled by the Sprit. The Christian leaders' mind, emotions, will, and physical strength all become available for the Spirit to guide and use. Under the Spirit's control, natural gifts of leadership are lifted to their highest power, sanctified for holy purpose. The truth for me is that God puts super on natural and divine purpose comes into being in the life of the leader. The Holy Spirit takes over where nature can go no further. Every text has a context and every leader has one as well.

Every leader must understand the context in which they are leading. Leading is only leading when there are followers. True leadership does not force anyone to follow. The life and ability of the leader inspires people to follow them. To inspire means to move someone to do something they want to do. It has a lot to do with helping people reach inside of themselves to pull out their creativity. Kouzer and Posner (2012) say:

> Exemplary leaders don't impose their vision of the future on people; they liberate the vision that's already stirring in their constituents. They awaken dreams, breathe life in to them, and arouse the belief that people can achieve something grand. When they communicate a shared vision, they bring these ideals into the conversation.

I love what Kouzes and Posner say about not imposing the vision on people but liberating the vision in people. Spiritual leadership calls for the leader to rely on the Holy Spirit to guide them as they lead. Only through the divine guidance of the Holy Spirit can leaders help their followers reach their greatest potential. It takes prayer, time, and reading to get the leader to a place of spiritual maturity that will sustain their level of responsibility. Of the three I would say that the foundation is definitely a rooted and grounded prayer life. According to Sanders (2007):

The spirit's help in prayer is mentioned in the Bible more frequently than any other help He gives us. All true praying comes from the Spirit's activity in our souls. Both Paul and Jude teach that effective prayer is "praying in the Spirit." That phrase means that we pray along the same lines, about the same things, in the same name, as the Holy Spirit.

Prayer changes people and things. When a spiritual leader relies heavily on prayer their connection to the Holy Spirit is quite noticeable. When it comes to time and reading, they are both very important things to give your attention to. Time is fleeting and so often we can get distracted and leave some major things undone. Reading allows spiritual leaders to continue to learn and grow. Prayer, good time management, and quality reading will help to shape a true spiritual leader.

Improving Leadership

Leadership has a lot to do with learning over time. A true spiritual leader transforms along the way. According to Dean (2010) Christians believe that transformation belongs to God, Christian formation—the patterning of our lives and our communities after Christ's self-giving love —requires grace, not determination. It is in following Jesus that we learn to love him; it is in participating in the mission of God that God changes us into disciples. Spiritual leaders are vessels of service who have chosen to be servant leaders. When I think about my own ability to lead I know that it is only through the grace and love of God that I am able to do what I do. As I change into the person that God calls me to be the people that I lead will change into the people that God called them to be. It is important to understand that change is difficult for many people and the leader sets the tone for how change happens. I remember many times where I had to be the *thermostat* of the group. I say that to mean that I regulated the emotion and intellect of the group. What I said and what I did had a direct impact on what the group was able to accomplish. The leader is not the reason for the group's success or failure. The leader is the catalyst for change that fosters the collective success or failure of the group. Spiritual leaders understand that the motivating force behind most groups is the passion of the participants. People are moved by what is in their hearts to do. It is the leader's responsibility to find out what the heart of the group is and then help them bring it to fruition. Spiritual leadership in conjunction with Alpha leadership is the change women in leadership need to cultivate.

Alpha Leadership principles, skills, and tools support effective interactions between leaders, co-workers, goals and the larger system in which they are acting. According to Dilts (2002) the Alpha Leadership model addresses each of these elements, which make up the "work space" of leadership, through what is referred to as the "triple As" of leadership: Anticipate, Align and Act. Anticipating has to do with the leader's ability to be aware of the larger system in which he or she and the team or organization are acting. Aligning has to do with the way a leader engages and interacts with others—achieving congruence in his or her own values and desires, and the values and desires of others in order to act effectively in pursuit of business goals and outcomes. Acting relates to establishing what is important to achieve the business goals, and making the commitment to persist in areas that make a difference through clarity and constancy of purpose. The triple "A's" of leadership that comprise Alpha Leadership (Anticipate,

Align, and Act) from a spiritual perspective can be found throughout Proverbs 31. The portrait of a woman in Proverbs 31 is a Spiritual Alpha Leader. The characteristics, attributes, and values of this woman is a model that any woman in leadership can find herself.

Your Lesson: Be a Woman who Honors God

Faith builds faith. When it comes to spiritual leadership the faith of the follower becomes a direct reflection of the faith of the leader. So often spirituality becomes the afterthought of leadership. Spirituality must be at the forefront of what it means to be a leader who desires to be God driven. Spiritual leadership involves intentional transformation in the life of the leader. Transformation involves an internal change with an external expression of that change. Although in general change can be defined as a person being different than s/he was previously, the word alone does not address how this difference manifests. Transformation, however gives the word change a spiritual illumination in that it unfolds the relative faith change that a person determines to be better than how they were previously. For the spiritual leader who is spirit-filled, they are continually transforming into the image of Christ. Sider (2007) says:

> The last verse of 2 Corinthians 3 is one of the most powerful statements about the sanctification that Paul expects of Christians and knows is possible in Christ: "And all of us, with unveiled faces, seeing the glory of the Lord as through reflected in a mirror, are being transformed into the same image from one degree of glory to another" (NRSV) Genuine Christians look directly into the face of Christ. The result? We are transformed into the very likeness of Christ! Not all at once, to be sure. The present tense-*we are being transformed*- indicates an ongoing process of sanctification. Day by day we are slowly becoming more and more like him. We do not expect absolute perfection now. But there is no room whatsoever in this verse for Christians to continue year after year in the same sin, repeating a ritual confession every week and making no progress in holiness.

Spiritual leadership calls for a transformation journey that happens on a daily basis. As the leader transforms the Spirit of God continues to provide new and innovative ideas to keep the vision moving forward.

Spiritual Position of Attention

Enjoyment of a Leader

ENJOY WHERE YOU ARE AS GOD REVEALS WHERE YOU ARE GOING

Wake up! Wake up! Clothe yourself with strength, O Zion! Put on your beautiful clothes, O Jerusalem, holy city! For uncircumcised and unclean pagans will no longer invade you. ² Shake off the dirt! Get up, captive Jerusalem! Take off the iron chains around your neck, O captive daughter Zion! ³ For this is what the LORD says: "You were sold for nothing, and you will not be redeemed for money." Isaiah 52:1-3 (NET)

Peace from God:_____

_____

_____

_____

_____

_____

My rest in God:_____

_____

_____

_____

_____

_____

My "yes" to God:_____

_____

_____

_____

_____

Afterword

Breathe my sister. I know you have taken in a lot of information. Your emotions have been on the craziest roller coaster of your life. I have messed up your theology on so many levels. Yet you are still reading and still standing. That means to me that something I have said has touched your soul. There has been a shift in your thinking and emotions, now what, now how, now who, now when? Letty Russell (1988) talks at length about what she calls inclusive theology. There are three shifts to inclusive theology where she says, inclusive theology first requires us to shift our attention from the Bible and tradition to people's stories. Second we have to move from a passive reception of the traditions to an active construction of our own theology. Third, doing our own theology requires moving away from a unified theological discourse to a plurality of voices and a genuine catholicity. Russell has helped me to understand that multiple voices must tell the universal story. The inference that women were not created in the image and likeness of God is unmistakably damaging to their spiritual growth and development. I am so blessed to have been enlightened by all that my eyes have seen, my ears have heard, and my heart has felt on my journey to womanist theology.

My life has changed, my mind has shifted, and my ministry will never be the same. I learned that feminist theology does not speak to the totality of my experience as a woman. There was something about it that included my experience as a woman but not a Black woman. I found myself more in line with womanist theology. According to Williams (1995) womanist theology is:

A prophetic voice concerned about the well-being of the entire African-American community, male and female, adults and children. Womanist theology attempts to help black women see, affirm, and have confidence in the importance of their experience and faith for determining the character of the Christian religion in the African-American community. Womanist theology challenges all oppressive forces impeding black women's struggle for survival and for the development of a positive, productive quality of life conducive to women's and the family's freedom and well-being. Womanist theology opposes all oppression based on race, sex, class, sexual preference, physical ability, and caste.

My spiritual journey resonates with Williams' understanding about theology from a Black woman's perspective. While I appreciate the feminist movement, it was not set in motion nor was it fueled by a collective restoration of all women. Katie G. Cannon (1985) says the result of Black women's historical effort is the cultivation of three virtues-invisible dignity, quiet grace, and unshouted courage-that characterize activities through which Black women determine their means to survive. Although Cannon is specifically speaking about Black women, the truth of what she is saying crosses ethnicity and speaks to the average woman's struggle. Invisible dignity includes induced compliance and docility in an effort to inculcate character traits necessary to determine appropriate responses to threats of physical and emotional violence. Quiet grace is the persistent struggle for human dignity in defiance of degrading oppression. And finally, unshouted courage is the capacity to constantly confront threats to survival in the face of reprisals of one's determination to survive. I believe that invisible dignity comes into play for women whenever they are forced to measure their worth against the standards set up to make them fall short. Quiet grace happens when condescension is the underlying presupposition in women's encounter with men as well as with women. A person does not have to tell you to be quiet to silence you. One word of condescension, two words of belittlement, or three words of dismissal can all silence. Unshouted courage is evident in the daily lives of women who struggle to pave the way for the younger generation of women through their faith and commitment to God.

My sisters, transformation is coming. It is time to embrace all of who God created you to be. Bradberry and Greaves (2009) suggest:

> Quit treating your feelings as good or bad; observe the ripple effect from your emotions; lean into your discomfort; feel your emotions physically; know who and what pushes your buttons; watch yourself like a hawk; keep a journal about your emotions; don't be fooled by a bad mood; don't be fooled by a good mood either; stop and ask yourself why you do the things you do; visit your values; check yourself; spot your emotions in books, movies, and music; seek feedback; and get to know yourself under stress.

Know who you are and what pushes your buttons. Start asking yourself why do I do what I do and what is most important to me? I am intentional about allowing God to transform me. Transformation is an outward manifestation of an inward change. Who I am becoming keeps me in the never ending cycle of change. As I live my life I encounter various experiences that foster this change. Transformation is about exploring the nature of being. It is about understanding, accepting, and implementing the change that is relative to the individual going through the transformation. God has taken me on such an amazing journey. I have been transformed spiritually, emotionally, and intellectually.

I am convinced that transformation is an ongoing process. Each transformative experience has shaped the next experience. My faith has taught me to look for those transformative moments and use them to make my life better. Self-awareness strategies help me to monitor my progression or regression. I have become a sagacious judge of what is transforming me and what is not. Prayer is one thing that has truly transformed my life. According to Henri Nouwen (2010) the discipline of prayer is the intentional, concentrated, and regular effort to create space for God. I can remember being young and praying because that is what I was taught. I watched the senior saints pray with intentionality which drew everyone emotionally. It took some time for me to realize that prayer is a personal experience that occurs as you talk to God. It keeps me self-aware of when I make the split second decision to shrink back instead of stand in the fullness of who I am. Even in writing this book, I have found subtle instances where I choose to shrink. The good news is now I am aware and make mid-course corrections. I am able to reframe my thinking right in the moment and it has changed my life. Humans have an amazing ability to reframe what they see and hear. Information can be internalized and either embraced or rejected. The amazing thing is that women have the ability to internalize negativity and have it control their lives, and even when they learn the truth they are still controlled by the negative imagery that was externally imposed. As I learn more about myself I am amazed at how much I did not know about me. I am continuously learning the art of the evolution of woman. I am proud to be an advocate for women and as I continue on this journey through womanist thought my understanding about our struggle expands.

When I think about how we interpret the Bible and the finality of the sayings, "Don't take anything from it and don't add anything to it" and "God said it, I believe it, and that's final", I am sad to say that I have participated in the marginalization of women unaware. Although change is difficult, it is necessary. Change must happen; those willing to go through the process will see that change may bring conflict, and conflict is not always negative. Conflict brought Eve into existence, conflict brought Miriam to the forefront, conflict brought Abigail to a place of Queen, conflict made Mary the mother of our Lord and Savior Jesus Christ, and conflict brought you to read this book. I have come to a place where I understand, something as simple as beginning my prayers with the God of Eve, Sarah, Rebekah, Leah and Rachael, is very empowering. I can also use more inclusive language and more feminine imagery. I have always been on board with black theology and I realized that black hermeneutics and feminist hermeneutics share a foundational truth. Both hermeneutic approaches begin with oppression and seek to liberate the truth of the Bible. As I walk in my liberation I can do nothing less than reach back and take all those willing to go, with me.

My sisters, we continue to walk in invisible dignity, quiet grace, and unshouted courage. Every time we shrink back into the fakeness of who we are to accommodate the men and women in our lives we lose a piece of ourselves. It is time for us to take a long hard look at what we have been taught about being a woman and being a leader. Our presence has been evident throughout the Bible. The misinterpretation and misrepresentation of who we are has held us hostage long enough. According to Gunnar (1962) look at history for a change, through the eyes of the people least visible in the record, search for the traces of people who are not there in the record but who were there. Ask how some things came to be that should not have been, how other things came to be in spite of much that hindered their being; and what things have yet to be, whose right to be must be asserted. As we stand in the fullness of who we are as Spiritual Alpha Females, let us consider the hard road of our foremothers and make an amazing trail for the generations coming behind us. Come out of the shadows women, it is time to shine.

Keep Shining On: A Letter to My Sisters
Inspired by Matthew 5:16

By Chaplain Judy Malana from *Soul Sisters: Devotions for and from African American, Latina, and Asian Women*, published by Tarcher-Penguin, an imprint of Penguin Random House, 2016

My Dearest Sisters,

Thank you.
Thank you for who you are.
Thank you for stepping out on a journey of faith.

Maybe you didn't always know it, but I have looked to you for encouragement.
When my own spiritual path wasn't so clear, I would lift my head and see you.
You have set the example for me, and so many others.

Whatever you have set your mind on you have accomplished.
From dreaming new dreams, to redefining yourself, to shattering stereotypes,
You have allowed the grace of God to move through you in magnificent ways.

Even when critics assailed, you stood firm.
When God opened doors for you, some minds remained closed
Yet you remained strong-not shackled by the prejudice of others.

When obstacles came, you pushed through
Never allowing the walls of self-doubt or fear to enclose you.
You never wavered from your calling.

You created sacred spaces in chaotic places
Even when the cell phone didn't stop ringing or the laundry remained undone,
Or when a sister needed someone to chat with awhile

You found refuge in positive relationships
And in not in places for pity parties or tirades
Each and every time the Lord was with you.

Phenomenal. Yes, you are.
From your inner strength to your fashion sense and fresh mani-
pedi
Your beauty illuminates the darkest night.
Keep shining on, my dear sisters.
You were not meant to stand in the shadows of others but to
Radiate the light God has given you.

Continue to blaze. You are not alone.
As doors of opportunity open, continue to walk through them.
There is no one or not thing that can stifle your steps.

Not when your sisters have your back
Yes, we are all on the sacred path together
Look around we are there.

The color of our skin, the texture of our hair, or the shape of our
hips
Do not matter-For we are all sisters.
United by the Spirit in a courageous journey of faith and action.

We are proving our critics wrong,
Pushing back against micro-inequities, micro-aggressions, and
micro-minded mentalities
We are letting our light shine on to glory of God.

Our time to exhale will come when we no longer have to justify
our place
On the field, at the table, or in the boardroom
Our victory is not ours alone, but belongs to our children and our
children's children

My dear sisters, we need each other

The road ahead is unchartered, and the journey is fierce, but God's grace is moving and working among us.

The Synergy of our Sisterhood is greater than the sum of our individual efforts.

And it is awesome.

Love and Peace,

Your Sister

References

Aronson, E. (1969). The theory of cognitive dissonance: A current perspective. Advances in Experimental Social Psychology, 4, 1-34

Bass, B. M., & Stogdill, R. M. (1990). Bass & Stogdill's handbook of leadership: Theory research, and managerial applications (3rd ed.). New York: Free Press.

Bergman, J. (2000) "The History of the teaching of human female inferiority in Darwinism" in *Answers in Genesis* Volume 14 Issue 1

Bradberry, T., & Greaves, J. (2009). Emotional intelligence 2.0. San Diego, CA: TalentSmart

Brenner, M. (2008). It's all about people: change management's greatest lever. *Business Strategy   Series, 9*(3).

Cannon, K. (1985) The Emergence of Black Feminist Consciousness" in Letty M Russell, ed., Feminist Interpretation of the Bible. Philadelphia: Westminster.

David, S., & Congleton, C. (2015). Emotional Agility. In D.

Goleman (Ed.), *HBR's 10 Must Reads On Emotional Intelligence.* Boston, MA: Harvard Business Review Press.

Dean, Kenda C. (2010). "The Almost-Chrisitan Formation of Teens: Faith, Nice and Easy" in Almost Christian: What the Faith of Our Teenagers Is Telling the American Church, published by Oxford University Press; used by permission of the publisher.

Deering, A., Dilts, R., Russell, J. (2002) Alpha Leadership: Tools for Business Leaders Who Want More From Life. New York: John Wiley & Sons.

Doll, D. (August 16, 2017), *Spiritual Injury* in "Healing the Storm: Finding Spiritual Peace in the Midst of One's Trauma.

Dowling, C. (1981). *The Cinderella Complex: A Women's Hidden Fear of Independence.* New York: Pocketbooks.

Ehrman, B, (2006). *Peter, Paul, and Mary Magdalene: The Followers of Jesus in History and Legend.* New York: Oxford Press

Festinger, L. (1957). A theory of cognitive dissonance. Standford, CA: Stanford University Press.

Flint, B. (2012). *The Journey to Competitive Advantage Through Servant Leadership.* Bloomington, IN: WestBow Press.

Gebara, I. (2002). *Out of the Depths: Women's Experience of Evil and Salvation.* Minneapolis: Fortress Press.

Goleman, D., Byatzis, R., & McKee, A. (2013). Primal leadership: Unleashing the power of emotional intelligence. Boston, MA: Harvard Business Review Press.

Greenleaf, R. (2013). Servant Leadership [25th Anniversary Edition]: A Journey into the Nature of Legitimate Power and Greatness.

Gregory the Great, (1993) Homily 33; quoted from Susan Haskins, *Mary Magdalene: Myth and Metaphor* New York: Harcourt Brace and Co.,.

Hardy, K. V. (1995) "The Cultural Genogram: Key to Training Culturally Competent Family Therapists" in Journal of Marital and Family Therapy, Vol. 21, No. 3.

Heifetz, Ronald A. (1998). *Leadership without Easy Answers.* Harvard University Press.

Hersey, P., Blanchard, K., & Johnson, D. (2014). *Management of organizational behavior.* Delhi

Holy Bible

Keen, S. (1991) *Fire in the Belly: On Being a Man* New York: Bantam Books

Kouzes, James M., & Posner, Barry Z. (2012). *The Leadership Challenge, 5th edition.* Jossey-Bass.

Mayer, J. D., Caruso, D., & Salovey, P. (1999). Emotional intelligence meets traditional standards for an intelligence. *Intelligence, 27,* 267-298.

McKenzie, V.M. (2002) Journey to the Well. Chicago: Urban Ministries Inc.

Myers, C. (2000) *Women in Scripture.* Grand Rapids, Michigan: William B. Eerdmans Publishing.

Myrdal, G. (1962) *An American Dilemma: The Negro Problem and Modern Democracy.* New York: Harper& Row.

Northouse, P. G. (2013). *Leadership: Theory and practice*, 6th edition. Sage Publishing.

Nouwen, H. J. M. (2010) *Spiritual Formation: Following the Movements of the Spirit*. New York: Harper Collins Publishing.

Paul, J. *Violence and the Sacred in America: A History of Domination*

Raver, M. (1998) *Listen To Her Voice: Women of the Hebrew Bible* San Francisco: Chronicle Books.

Rhodes, Lynn N. *Co-Creating: A Feminist Vision of Ministry*. Philadelphia: Westminster Press, 1987.

Rodin, R. Scott. (2010). *The Steward Leader*. InterVarsity Press Academic

Rogers, Katherine M. *The Troublesome Helpmate: A History of Misogyny in Literature*. University of Washington Press, 1966.

Rose, Stephen C. (1996) *The Grass Roots Church: A Manifesto for Protestant Renewal*. New York: Holt, Pinehart, & Winston.

Rosenbach, William E., Robert L. Taylor, and Mark A. Youndt. (2012). *Contemporary Issues in Leadership*. Westview Press.

Rosser, S. V. (1992) *Biology and Feminism; A Dynamic Interaction*, New York: Twayne Publishing

Russell, Letty M. *Inheriting Our Mothers' Gardens: Feminist Theology in Third World Perspective*. Philadelphia: The Westminster Press, 1988.

Sanders, Oswald J. (2006). *Spiritual Leadership: Principles of Excellence for Every Believer*. Moody Publishers.

Schaberg, J (2003) *The Resurrection of Mary Magdalene: Legends, Apocrypha, and the Christian Testament* New York: Continuum.

Sider, R. J. (2005). The Scandal of the Evangelical Conscience, Why Are Christians Living Just Like the Rest of the World. Grand Rapids: Baker Books.

Teubal, S. J. (1990) *Hagar the Egyptian: The Lost Tradition of the Matriarchs.* San Francisco: Harper.

Williams, D S. (1995) *Sisters in the Wilderness: The Challenge of Womanist God-Talk.* Maryknoll, New York: Orbis Books

Other Books By Dr. Lang

Does Love Cover....THAT?: The Healing Process of the Fruit of the Spirit

Does Love Cover....THAT?: The Workbook

Finding Me: A Woman's Theology of Self- Identification

Beside the Still Waters: Having Faith Even When...

The Chick on the Side: From the Heart of a Wife

A Conversation With Myself: Healing the Internal Voice